PUBLIC VOICES

Literature and Politics
with special reference to the Seventeenth Century

By the same Author

★

DRAMA AND SOCIETY IN THE AGE OF JONSON

EXPLORATIONS

FURTHER EXPLORATIONS

SOME SHAKESPEAREAN THEMES

AN APPROACH TO HAMLET

POETRY, POLITICS AND THE ENGLISH TRADITION

PUBLIC VOICES

LITERATURE AND POLITICS
WITH SPECIAL REFERENCE TO
THE SEVENTEENTH CENTURY

The Clark Lectures
for 1970-71

L. C. KNIGHTS

ROWMAN AND LITTLEFIELD
TOTOWA, N.J.

Published by
Chatto & Windus Ltd
40 William IV Street
London WC2

*

First published in the United States of America, 1972
by Rowman and Littlefield, Totowa, N.J.

ISBN 0 87471 081 2

Printed in Great Britain

For
Harry and Elsie Barnes

CONTENTS

PREFACE

THE five lectures which follow were delivered at Cambridge in February and March, 1971, as the Clark Lectures for 1970-71. I wish to thank the Master and Fellows of Trinity College for inviting me to give them.

I must offer here a short explanation and apology. My full title should have been: 'Some aspects of the relationship between literature and politics, with special reference to some selected authors of the seventeenth century'. Clearly that would not do; but I should explain here the limits of the task I have set myself. I shall not attempt an assessment of the immediate political content of works of literature in the seventeenth century, as Miss C. V. Wedgwood did in the Clark Lectures for 1958, published as *Poetry and Politics under the Stuarts*. Nor shall I attempt a detailed analysis of significant relationships and contrasts between the language used in works of all kinds that have a political content—plays, poems, treatises, tracts, speeches and so on within this period: that would be far beyond my powers. All I propose is to raise some questions, and make some suggestions, about the ways in which an interest in literature and an interest in politics may usefully be brought together, taking my illustrations from such writings as I have had the inclination, and the leisure, to read. Even this modest aim has its obvious hazards. To succeed in it would require not only an extensive knowledge of the literature of the seventeenth century, but of the more or less formal political thought of the time, and of the details of its politics; and the ideal undertaker would also be someone with some direct knowledge of the workings of politics in his own day. In a university where specialists abound the trespasser is always uncomfortably aware of gamekeepers and man-traps. But one of the functions of a university is to promote the art of intelligent trespassing. To put it more formally, the university is not only a place where various specialisms are cultivated; it is, or should be, a place where there is at least some opportunity for creative interplay between the different disciplines. If anything said here should help forward that kind of enterprise, or should encourage any students to go further along the lines that I shall sketch, I shall be more than satisfied.

Some of the material included here was used in two Lewis Fry Lectures at Bristol University (Spring, 1970), in three public lectures in the University of London (Autumn, 1970), and in the three public lectures that I gave as Mrs William Beckman Visiting Professor in the University of California, Berkeley, during the Spring Quarter, 1970. This is an opportunity to express sincere thanks for the warm hospitality—and more than that— that my wife and I received during our visit to Berkeley. We owe a special debt of gratitude to the Chairman of the English Department and his wife—John and Marie Jordan.

The lectures are published substantially as delivered, keeping the spoken form. A few paragraphs omitted for lack of time have been restored to the text. Since this is not a work of scholarship I have kept footnotes and references to a minimum. But I have tried to make it easy for the common reader to look up important quotations; and I have, I hope, acknowledged all my debts. I am grateful to my son, Ben Knights, for checking the proofs.

L. C. KNIGHTS

Queens' College, Cambridge
April 1971

CHAPTER ONE

The Language of Politics: Some
Questions Raised

(i)

A MAIN purpose of these lectures is to suggest the importance of literature and the study and enjoyment of literature for the health of our political life: no less. As a teacher of literature—as someone, that is, whose main function is to help keep alive the masterpieces, great and small, that help us to find our humanity —I have therefore an axe to grind: I want to bring out the value of my own pursuits in relation to the field of public affairs. It is as well that I should show that I am aware of the dangers. It was Yeats who, speaking for the poets, said, 'We have no gift to set a statesman right': poets and students of poetry are no more likely to be 'right' about particular political issues than those whose main interests lie elsewhere. 'Those who quit their proper character, to assume what does not belong to them,' said Burke, 'are, for the greater part, ignorant both of the character they leave, and of the character they assume. Wholly unacquainted with the world with which they are so fond of meddling, and inexperienced in all its affairs, on which they pronounce with so much confidence, they have nothing of politics but the passions they excite.' This rebuke to the radical Dissenters of the Old Jewry is something we all need to keep in mind—but as a word of caution, not as a No Trespass notice that we are compelled to observe. It is of course true that very few of us

11

have much direct experience of the intricacies and practical difficulties of decision-making in politics, with all the various kinds of knowledge—economic and diplomatic knowledge, as well as knowledge gained in the hurly-burly of competing interests—that this involves. It is only too easy for, say, a professor of English who writes on Shakespeare's political wisdom to appear a mere 'venerable state moralist', as Coleridge called Major Cartwright. But perhaps the mention of Coleridge—whose political insights are often so shrewd, and whose thinking about the state is after all not unrelated to his thinking about poetry—may remind us that things are not so simple as they may appear to practical men.

To approach politics from the point of view of the student of literature is of course open to another objection, or what may at first seem to be such. What literature continually brings home to us is the value of the individual consciousness and the living moment. As students of literature we are concerned with values embodied in particular works and directly experienced: we are concerned with the realm of ends. Political activity, though necessary, is a means to an end. Politics, moreover, by their very nature tend towards abstraction and simplification; and the slogans and abstractions of politics can have a fearful power. Leonard Woolf, in the volume of his autobiography called *Downhill all the Way: an Autobiography of the Years 1919 to 1939*, writes of the Soviet purges of the 1930s, and of two men he knew who disappeared in them:

> Power and the struggle for power are of course realities involved in the machinery of communism and Soviet Russia in which Rothstein and Mirsky became fatally involved; but power is always the concern of a tiny minority. The Rothsteins and Mirskys and the thousands of anonymous victims of communism are sacrificed for words and phrases, tales 'told by an idiot, full of sound and fury, signifying nothing'.

That has the understandable bitterness of a man who has seen friends caught and crushed in an inhuman machine. But take a more general statement of a similar attitude by a man who spent his life exploring the nature of human consciousness and expressing in words and paint his vision of what it means to be human. In a Note-book entry of *c.* 1810, Blake wrote:

> I am really sorry to see my Countrymen trouble themselves about Politics. If Men were Wise, the Most arbitrary Princes could not hurt them. If they are not wise, the Freest Government is compell'd to be a Tyranny. Princes appear to me to be Fools. Houses of Commons & Houses of Lords appear to me to be fools; they seem to me to be something Else besides Human Life.[1]

We need not trouble ourselves about the apparent—and it is only apparent—attitude of quiescence towards arbitrary government. Blake had been, and continues to be, a pretty effective opponent of any kind of tyranny. ('The strongest poison ever known Came from Caesar's Laurel Crown.') The point is simply that compared with the direct human import of art and the artist's realm of values, politics must often seem to be not only 'a second-rate form of human activity' (the phrase is Michael Oakeshott's*), but 'something else besides human life'. Why, then, should we take notice of the artist—who with at least part of himself must remain uncommitted to programmes and policies—when he chooses to write about politics, which inevitably deal in the immediate pressure of interests and social passions? To ask the question is to answer it, and to dispose of the objection. It is because the artist is concerned with values in the realm 'beyond politics' that, whatever his own political commitments, he can remind us of the ends that politics are intended to

* See the Introduction to his edition of Hobbes' *Leviathan*, p. lxiv.

serve—that is of course to the extent that he remains an artist and does not turn mere propagandist. The problem is how to make the connexion intelligible, and to suggest how it may, or should be, effective.

To do this will necessarily involve other matters, to which we shall come presently. Meanwhile there is one other preliminary point to make. It is abundantly clear that we can't keep our interest in literature pure and uncontaminated by political interests: the writers themselves won't let us. The anonymous editor of my copy of Stendhal's *Lucien Leuwen** quotes from Stendhal's own *Racine et Shakespeare*: 'Toute idée politique dans un ouvrage de littérature . . . est comme un coup de pistolet au milieu d'un concert'. But the editor very properly comments: 'En fait, si l'on ôte la politique de *Le Rouge et le Noir*, *La Chartreuse de Parme* ou *Lucien Leuwen* tout l'édifice s'écroule'. As for the literature of our own country, we all know how many creative writers—from Langland to Dryden, and from Dryden to Conrad—have dealt powerfully with political themes. Shakespeare's English Histories are political plays; so are *Julius Caesar* and *Coriolanus*; political debate forms an important part of *Troilus and Cressida*. And if we say that politics has to do with the distribution and the grounds of power in society, then clearly although neither *King Lear* nor *Macbeth* nor *The Tempest* are political plays in any narrow sense, it is also clear that they have political implications. When, in the Putney Debates of 1647, Colonel Rainborough said, 'For really I think that the poorest he that is in England has a life to live, as the greatest he', he put succinctly one of the truths that *King Lear* brings home to our imaginations.

This however is only a reminder. My brief account in

* Editions Baudelaire (1966).

the lectures that follow of the relations between literature and politics in the seventeenth century will not deal—or will deal only in a passing and subordinate way—with the political *content* of particular works and their relation to immediate issues of their day. What I most want you to think about is *the nature of political language, of ways of talking about politics.* It is when we focus our attention there that we may best bring out how far such a study is from being only of historical interest. Indeed, both as students of literature and students of history, we need to clear our minds about certain general issues that are best raised in the context of our own present.

What needs to be said is simple enough. When politics are conducted in bad or corrupted language they are not properly conducted. What I mean by bad language in this respect can be illustrated by the mid-term manifestos of the two major political parties in October, 1968 (with some glances forward to the more nearly contemporary). The Labour manifesto (as reported in *The Times*, September 30, 1968) showed a tendency to slide into abstractions. Dealing with the difficult question of relations between the advanced industrial nations and the developing countries, it says:

> We intend to search for fresh solutions on an international scale—world food boards, staple commodity agreements, and further progress in the creation of a sound liquidity position —linking the creation of drawing rights with aid to the developing countries.

This of course has a meaning for economists; but the manifesto is addressed to ordinary men and women who are asked to support particular economic arrangements, and I suspect that for most of them 'a sound liquidity position' remains a mere blur. They have a right to ask that 'a sound liquidity position' should be 'cashed' into terms they can handle and think with. Abstractions muffle the reality of whatever is being discussed: they lull the reader in ways that can be dangerous. In February, 1970, Mr Healey, Secretary of State for Defence in the last Labour government, remarked: 'The purpose of nuclear weapons as we see them is to restore the credibility of the overall deterrent in a situation in which a large-scale conventional attack shows that that credibility has disappeared' (*The Times*, February 24, 1970). What a demonic bang is muffled here! 'Why do you mince the matter? Why not name the thing?'—as Cobbett said of the clause about 'corporal infliction', meaning flogging, in the Mutiny Act of 1811. The manifesto continued:

> Perhaps the greatest new factor in British politics is the present obsolescence of many aspects of our institutions. This has led to alienation from disillusion with those institutions.

The word 'alienation' has had a considerable history since Marx used it: it would be interesting to know what exactly the authors of the manifesto had in mind. Whatever they intended, it is, to say the least, difficult for the reader to be very actively engaged in this languid movement of abstractions: 'the greatest factor ... is the ... obsolescence of many aspects ...'. It is not merely that phrases and tropes are shoddy by some assumed 'literary standards'—'A population time-bomb is now ticking around us' (what brave member of the Fire Service will pick it up and throw it in the sea?)—it is that this language is wholly inadequate for discussion of the ends that economic and political arrangements are meant to serve, or for examining with real understanding the relation between means and ends.

In the Conservative manifesto the vices of style were rather different. Perhaps we may overlook a few examples of the sham dramatic—as when a man forced to seek employment away from a place where he might well want to live is said to be moving 'to another and *more challenging* job in another part of Britain'; or when it is stated not simply that our foreign debts are perhaps dangerously high, but that 'the Government, *cap in hand*, have run up foreign debts . . . which it will take years to repay'. But here too there is a certain muffling of important questions. This time they are not clouded in abstractions like 'the obsolescence of . . . aspects': they are simply hidden by a language that pretends to a forthrightness that the facts do not allow. 'What Britain needs is to release the energies and abilities of the people. That means allowing achievement to get its reward.' (What kind of achievement? And what kinds of reward, if any, are in question besides the possible financial ones?) 'Our tax changes will give incentive and reward enterprise.' (Again, what sort of enterprise?) 'The Conservative Party is the party of free enterprise. It is also the party of choice.' (On which one reflects that some kinds of choice depend on the money you have in your pocket, on the education you have had, and so on. It was, I believe, Anatole France who said, 'Rich and poor are equal in law, for both alike are forbidden to sleep under arches'.)[2]

The questions raised here are not merely political ones, even though, as Mr Ian Robinson has reminded us, 'The quality of the discourse is the quality of the national political life'.* Political language is part of a wider public language, and I think that, whatever our political affilia-

* Ian Robinson, 'The Extinction of British Politics', *Oxford Review*, No. 7 (Hilary Term, 1968). See also George Orwell, 'Politics and the English Language', in *Inside the Whale*.

tions, we should take very seriously what Mr Herbert Marcuse has said about 'the closing of the universe of discourse'.* In the handling of public matters in the mass media we find, he claims, 'the language of total administration'—a language that in vocabulary, syntax and general manner blocks any movement of the mind towards reflection and criticism. Of the language 'that orders and organizes, that induces people to do, to buy and to accept', Marcuse says: 'It is transmitted in a style which is a veritable linguistic creation; a syntax in which the structure of the sentence is abridged and condensed in such a way that no tension, no "space", is left between the parts of the sentence.' Moving in synonyms and tautologies, it 'precludes genuine development of meaning', and 'repels demonstration, qualification, negation of its codified and declared meaning'. Even fundamental contradictions are welded together into units of language that repel criticism—'clean bomb', 'harmless fall-out'.†[3] With this operational language—'radically antihistorical', because history which reveals alternative possibilities is dangerous—Marcuse contrasts the true language of consciousness. This, with its implicit appeal to something beyond brute assertion, an invitation to some kind of dialectical play, 'breaks open a closed universe of discourse and its petrified structures. The key terms of this language are not hypnotic nouns which evoke endlessly the same frozen predicates. They rather allow of an open development.' If, then, we regard with suspicion the language of the mass media it is not because it offends against our canons of taste, but because, in Chomsky's

* Herbert Marcuse, *One-Dimensional Man*, Chapter iv.

† Compare Orwell: 'Political writing in our time consists almost entirely of prefabricated phrases bolted together like the pieces of a child's Meccano set'. —*Op. cit.*

phrase, it leads to 'the narrowing of the range of the thinkable'.*

I know of course that the dangers of which I have spoken are in some ways peculiar to the present day. I have used them because they seem to offer the most effective way of making a simple but very important point. Behind the public language of any age—or, if you like, the languages in which public and social issues are discussed—is a way of life, a 'life-style', with all that this implies by way of value and commitment.

Dr J. P. Stern, in an article in *The Times Literary Supplement* published shortly after the invasion of Czechoslovakia in the summer of 1968, wrote as follows:

> Two kinds of voices can be heard from the Czechoslovak radio stations. The first is the one that has been heard for twenty years now. It is monotonous, impersonal, an automaton voice going through phrases like 'normalization of conditions' or 'activation of imperialism's machinations against socialist countries' as though they belonged to the vocabulary of a strange tongue. It pronounces a sentence like 'the talks passed in an atmosphere of frankness, comradeship and friendship' with a tired indifference to its meaning . . .
>
> The other kind of voice has an intimacy, a calm and informal directness of address quite unlike that heard anywhere else. Its sentences are unstudied and impromptu, colloquial and unfaltering. Again and again it returns to the words, 'reason', 'realism' and 'truth'. Not fanatically, not as though these words were a magic formula of propitiation. The words are proffered with a slight didactic edge, as an invitation to consider a case the right and justice of which will surely be established and implemented.

Dr Stern went on to relate this use of an 'open' language appealing to reason to the belief in education and free

* Noam Chomsky, *American Power and the New Mandarins* (New York: Pantheon and Vintage Books, 1969; London: Chatto and Windus and Pelican Books, 1969), p. 133.

enquiry associated with such national figures as John Hus, Comenius and Thomas Masaryk. It was this that the Czechs were struggling for—the right to use this kind of language, and the conditions that make it possible to do so.*

(ii)

It is questions such as these that we need to have in mind when we consider the political and public language of any period of the past, both for the sake of our historical understanding and for the sake of what we can bring home and apply. There is however one further objection to anticipate. The examples I shall use are of very different kinds; and I may say in advance that I know very well that the language of debate is different from the language of a published manifesto, which in turn is different from that of a considered contribution to fundamental political thought; and all these are different from the language of a creative writer dealing with public themes. But there are certain general criteria which, with due allowance for differences of purpose, may be applied to all forms of speech and writing that offer to deal with political and public affairs. Indeed, a main point that I wish to make is that there should be *some* connexion—however complex and difficult to define—between the first three kinds (speech, manifesto, political theory) and the fourth (art). The nature of those criteria and the nature of the connexion is what I hope to suggest. And this in turn reveals

* *Times Literary Supplement*, September 5, 1968. Dr Stern's article gives force to Coleridge's remark, 'What a magnificent History of acts of individual minds, sanctioned by the collective Mind of the Country, a language is'.—Quoted by Alice D. Snyder, *Coleridge on Logic and Learning*, p. 138.

on the horizon a further, more difficult, question. 'State business is a cruel Trade: good nature is a Bungler in it', said Halifax. There is truth in that, but not the whole truth. It is at least an open question whether politics may not be brought into connexion with good nature, reason and imagination, the 'trade' being somewhat humanized thereby. Meanwhile our concern is speech and style, style as itself an effective agent in determining the political climate; and before turning to my seventeenth-century authors in the lectures that follow I should like to ask your attention for a few samples from other periods that may help us to see more clearly what we are looking for.

If a marked feature of today's public scene is language that *prevents* thought ('narrowing the range of the thinkable'), there is also, as we have seen, a public language that *dissipates* it. Both have in common a failure of grasp, a quality that moves the listener's or reader's attention away from the matter as it really is; both inflation and the language that seeks to compel are inseparable from distortion. Our current dangers—allowing for our ancestors' lack of sophistication in such matters—have therefore a long ancestry. A few examples must serve for many, for everyone with some knowledge of history and literature will be able to supply his own.

In 1835 Andrew Ure, professor of chemistry and writer on many scientific subjects,* published *The Philosophy of Manufactures*—partly a technical account of some of the new manufacturing processes, partly a rhapsody on the progress of unfettered technology and an attack on government interference (including the Corn Laws —'this expiring act of feudal despotism'). When Ure is not being severely technical he allows himself some

* He also inaugurated a course of popular scientific lectures for working-men in Glasgow, probably—according to the *D.N.B.*—the first of its kind.

licence in the substitution of figured speech for sober prose.

> In pursuing a gradually progressive but steady approach to a liberal system, we must tamper as little as possible with manufacturing or commercial industry by legislative regulation. Like love, its workings must be free as air; for at sight of human ties, it will spread the light wings of capital and fly away from bondage. By loosening the bands, in which the unwise tenderness of our old legislators had swaddled the trade of Great Britain, by letting it run wherever it may list, by exposing it freely to the breezes of competition, we have within a few years given it fresh vigour and a new life. National industry has the same principle of vigorous growth as the mountain pine. Self-sown in the clefts of the rocks, it creates a soil for its roots, shoots up a hardy stem, is invigorated by the gale which would blast the nursery plant, eventually rears its head on high, and forms a mast for some 'tall ammiral'. Planted in the rich compost of a parterre, having its infant shoots nursed in the close atmosphere of a forcing glass, protected from the extremes of heat, moisture, and drought by a watchful gardener, it remains feeble, dwarfish, and sickly, and never can become a mass of timber profitable to its owner, or useful to the state. The elements of industry may be expressed in one word—competition.*

This has some affinity with Macaulay's rhetoric on the practical benefits of the New Philosophy,† and as such has a certain period interest: it can't have done much harm except in inflating other wind-bags. But rhetoric of this kind is a device for not seeing, and when Ure turns his attention to the hours and conditions of work of children in the Lancashire cotton-mills the blindness of

* Andrew Ure, *The Philosophy of Manufactures, or an Exposition of the Scientific, Moral and Commercial Economy of the Factory System of Great Britain*, 1835 (Frank Cass, 1967), p. 453.

† I refer to the concluding paragraphs of his review (1830) of Southey's *Colloquies*.

the man is, so to speak, one with the defects of the writer. Of the children employed in cotton-spinning, he remarks:

> It was delightful to observe the nimbleness with which they pieced the broken ends [of the thread] as the mule-carriages began to recede from the fixed roller beams, and to see them at leisure, after a few seconds' exercise of their tiny fingers, to amuse themselves in any attitude they chose, till the stretch and winding-on were once more completed. The work of these lively elves seemed to resemble a sport, in which habit gave them a pleasing dexterity . . .
>
> 'When the carriages of [the mules] have receded a foot and a half or two feet from the rollers,' says Mr Tufnell, 'nothing is to be done, not even attention is required from either spinner or piecer.' Both of them stand idle for a time, and in fine spinning particularly, for three-quarters of a minute, or more. Consequently, if a child remains at this business twelve hours daily, he has nine hours of inaction. And though he attends two mules, he has still six hours of non-exertion. Spinners sometimes dedicate these intervals to the perusal of books. . . .*

Put beside this a passage from the first of Coleridge's two pamphlets in support of Sir Robert Peel's Bill (1818) to shorten the factory hours for children, who were then working from twelve to fifteen hours a day. One of the objections that Coleridge answers is 'that the proposed plan is a mere palliative better calculated to excite discontent in the sufferers, than to effect any considerable diminution of the evil'. He uses the analogy of 'a journey too long for the traveller's strength', in which 'it is the last few miles that torment him by fatigue and injure him by exhaustion'. He continues:

> Substitute [for the tired traveller, who at least has fresh air and a change of scene] a child employed on tasks the most

---

* *Op. cit.*, pp. 301, 309-10. The last extract is included in *Writing and Action, a Documentary Anthology*, compiled and edited by Mary Palmer (Allen and Unwin, 1938).

opposite to all its natural instincts, were it only from their improgressive and wearying uniformity—in a heated stifling atmosphere, fevered by noise and glare, both limbs and spirits outwearied—and that, at the tenth hour, he has still three, four, or five hours more to look forward to. Will he, will the poor little *sufferer*, be brought to believe that these hours are mere trifles—or the privilege of going home not worth his thanks? Generalities are apt to deceive us. Individualise the sufferings which it is the object of this Bill to remedy, follow up the detail in some one case with a human sympathy, and the deception vanishes.*

The passage suffers from extraction, for what distinguishes the pamphlets is the union of specific information, strict logic, and a basic humanity. But the main point is clear in the last sentence of the passage quoted: 'Generalities are apt to deceive us. *Individualise the sufferings which it is the object of this Bill to remedy, follow up the detail in some one case with a human sympathy, and the deception vanishes.*†

This comparison is not directed to the unnecessary task of demonstrating the superiority of Coleridge: it is intended to point to the criteria by which we distinguish good writing in a public cause from the less good or the bad. Intelligent conviction—like folly, obstinacy and the desire to manipulate—can express itself in many different ways. But we can learn to recognize the different tones that indicate difference of quality when we hear them. The formal name for this learning is literary criticism, which is as necessary for the historian or the student of

* Quoted from *Inquiring Spirit: a New Presentation of Coleridge from his Published and Unpublished Writings*, edited by Kathleen Coburn (1951), pp. 351-65.

† On Coleridge's 'attachment to experience', his insistence on 'the relations between personal instances and social institutions', see Raymond Williams, *Culture and Society, 1780-1950* (Penguin Books), pp. 81-2.

politics as it is for the reader of plays and novels. And the distinctions we arrive at need to be kept in mind even when we are dealing with the speeches and writings of great men.

A case in point is Burke. Burke is great because he continually reminds us of the wide scope of awareness necessary for the statesman, as opposed to the mere politician; because he is a lasting challenge to the simplifiers; because he offers a powerful demonstration that calculation based on abstraction is no substitute for the political wisdom that recognizes the connexion between the state as a political organ and the network of moral relations that constitute civil society. It is the organicism of Burke's thought—defining, among other things, the part played by tradition and sentiment in a creative response to the needs of the present—that makes the *Reflections on the Revolution in France* compulsory reading for those whose bias is towards political action as the expression of naked 'reason' and will alone.[4] But Burke too can mislead by falling into the same rhetorical traps against which, in other contexts, he warns so cogently. In other words, when he misleads his style betrays him.

It is necessary here to refer to the conclusion of the famous apostrophe to Marie Antoinette, though since it is so well known a few extracts will serve.

I thought ten thousand swords must have leaped from their scabbards to avenge even a look that threatened her with insult.—But the age of chivalry is gone.—That of sophisters, œconomists, and calculators, has succeeded; and the glory of Europe is extinguished for ever. Never, never more, shall we behold that generous loyalty to rank and sex, that proud submission, that dignified obedience, that subordination of the heart, which kept alive, even in servitude itself, the spirit of an exalted freedom. The unbought grace of life . . . the nurse of manly sentiment and heroic enterprize is gone! It is gone, that sensibility of principle, that chastity of honour, which felt a stain like a wound, which inspired courage whilst it mitigated ferocity, which ennobled whatever it touched, and under which vice itself lost half its evil, by losing all its grossness.

This mixed system of opinion and sentiment had its origin in the antient chivalry. . . . It is this which has given its character to modern Europe. It is this which has distinguished it under all its forms of government, and distinguished it to its advantage, from all the states of Asia. . . . It was this, which, without confounding ranks, had produced a noble equality, and handed it down through all the gradations of social life. It was this opinion which mitigated kings into companions, and raised private men to be fellows with kings. . . .

But now all is to be changed. All the pleasing illusion, which made power gentle, and obedience liberal, which harmonized the different shades of life, and which, by a bland assimilation, incorporated into politics the sentiments which beautify and soften private society, are to be dissolved by this new conquering empire of light and reason.*

In a valuable book, *The Language of Politics in the Age of Wilkes and Burke*, Dr James T. Boulton says of the section from which I have quoted,

the 'apostrophe' to the French Queen has a special function in acting as the centrepiece of the *Reflections*: it is central because it is the most memorable passage . . . and because it is central to the argument, the passage which gathers up the principal ideas Burke has previously expressed, invests them with a new quality, and then acts as a kind of supercharger for the argument that follows. At this rhetorical and philosophical centrepoint Burke's vision of moral disorder contrasted with the symbol of the moral order he venerates reaches climactic proportions, and the principles underlying his vision receive their most startling evocation.[5]

* *Reflections*, ed. O'Brien, pp. 170-1. It is only fair to add that immediately after this sorry stuff Burke rises again into genuine political philosophy.

26

All I can myself accept of this account is the word 'startling'. 'The age of chivalry'—however we define it, and with all its faults—contributed something of immense importance to the life of Europe; but did Burke really think that it was still alive in the age of Louis XV? Did he really think that the rural and urban poverty of his own country fostered 'the spirit of an exalted freedom'? (Cobbett or Clare or his own protégé Crabbe could have informed him better.) Did he really think that in France or in England in the seventeenth and eighteenth centuries 'a noble equality' was 'handed down through all the gradations of social life', that power was gentle, and that politics had incorporated 'the sentiments which beautify and soften private society'? Of course he didn't. Not one of his generalizations will stand the touch of specific historical knowledge; and to this, and a few other passages in the *Reflections* we can justly apply what Burke said elsewhere of 'the hocus-pocus of abstractions':

> Blessings on his soul that first invented sleep, said Don Sancho Panza the wise! All those blessings, and ten thousand times more, on him who found out abstraction, personification, and impersonals! In certain cases they are the first of all soporoficks.*

When we come to consider some different kinds of political writing in the period that runs from Shakespeare to Dryden—as indeed when we consider the political speeches and writings of any period—we shall be alert not only to what can be summarized as substance or argument; we shall be alert to tone and manner. We shall, to put it simply, be listening for the authentic voice of reason, humanity and common sense—the voice we hear (to take an example from another place and period) in

* *Letters on a Regicide Peace*, Letter IV; Burke, *Select Works*, ed. E. J. Payne, p. 267.

some of the speeches of Abraham Lincoln. Authentic voices, it is hardly necessary to say, do not speak as one voice. But to distinguish what *is* authentic—*not* simplifying, vague or bent only on asserting itself—is an essential part of the process by which we make present for ourselves the wisdom still available in the clash of dead factions—which is, to my mind, a major use of history. And if authentic voices are heard on different sides, they are also heard in places that the student of literature or the history of ideas is liable to overlook—for example, in some of the fumbling speeches of the Putney Debates of the Army in 1647.* It is, I should say, an authentic voice that we hear in the speech of Lord Digby when he proclaimed his opposition to the attainder of Strafford:

> I profess, I can have no notion of any bodies intent to subvert the Laws Treasonably, or by force; and this design of Force not appearing, all his other wicked Practises cannot amount so high with me.
>
> I can find a more easie and more natural Spring, from whence to derive all his other Crimes, than from an intent to bring in Tyranny, and to make his own Posterity, as well as Us, Slaves; as from Revenge, from Pride, from Avarice, from Passion, and insolence of Nature.
>
> But had this of the *Irish* Army been proved, it would have diffused a Complexion of Treason over all, it would have been a Withe, indeed, to bind all those other scattered and lesser branches, as it were, into a Faggot of Treason.
>
> I do not say but the rest may represent him a man as worthy to die, but perhaps worthier than many a Traytor. I do not say, but they may justly direct Us to Enact, That they shall be Treason for the future.
>
> But God keep me from giving Judgment of Death on any man, and of Ruine to his innocent Posterity, upon a Law made *a Posteriori*.
>
> Let the Mark be set on the door where the Plague is, and then let him that will enter die. . . .

* Printed in A. J. P. Woodhouse, *Puritanism and Liberty.*

The danger being so great, and the Case so doubtful, that I see the best Lawyers in diametral opposition concerning it: Let every man wipe his Heart, as he does his Eyes, when he would judge of a nice and subtile Object. The Eye if it be pretincted with any colour, is vitiated in its discerning. Let Us take heed of a blood-shotten Eye in Judgment.[6]

That Digby was inept and changeable as a statesman should not prejudice us here. He is trying to cut through an apparently inextricable tangle and to relate the case to basic principles of justice; he is against half-remembered and ambiguous evidence, against the new doctrine of 'cumulative treason',* against condemning a man on laws made *a posteriori*. It is a strong presumption of honesty of intention when a man uses, not formal eloquence, but homely and familiar metaphors and comparisons that disperse the fog of abstract argument and sum up in a sharp phrase the actualities of the case. And the striking imagery is in the service of a starkly stated principle of human justice. 'What are we going to do, with a Breath, either Justice or Murder' is something that, to decide, summons all the honesty a man has: 'Let us take heed of a blood-shotten eye in judgment'.

I have said that an authentic voice, however we define it, does not tell us all we need to know about a man, his public attitudes, or his particular policies. But it tells us something of great moment—far more, perhaps, than we commonly recognize. And if the authentic voices are various, they have in common certain qualities that we are accustomed to define in speaking of the imagination in works of literature. The nature of that connexion—and its importance for us, now—will receive some attention in the following lectures.

* Strafford is reported to have said that 'he never heard tell that thirty black rabbits made one black horse'.

CHAPTER TWO

Shakespeare

PAUL VALÉRY says somewhere that politics are the art of preventing people from meddling with what concerns them. There is much truth in that apparently cynical remark. The things that really concern us are of course things with which our connexion is personal and direct: fire and food, sea and sky, people, pictures and books that we care about—all these belong to the world that Martin Buber defined as the world of *I* and *Thou*, the world of relationship. But man cannot live exclusively in the world of *Thou*: there is also the world of *It*, the world that can be, has to be, manipulated and arranged, and that necessarily affects the quality of the personal world—what people have to eat or their opportunities for exploring the realms of thought and art, for example. Conflicting needs and desires have to be adjusted; and although in a small social group there is always the possibility of arrangement in the spirit of relationship, in larger social structures arrangement is inevitably a matter of the play of conflicting interests within the world of *It*. One name for large-scale arrangements of this kind is politics; and not only do politics involve some degree of domination rather than mutuality (decisions must be taken and orders given), the world of politics is to some extent a world of abstraction, the most extreme instances being seen in class and international rivalries. In a note to some of his poems, Yeats spoke of 'the futility of all discipline that is not of the whole being'; but, he added, 'political Ireland sees the good citizen but as a man who holds to certain opinions and not as a man of good will'. When opinion takes over there is a tendency, and often more than a tendency, for the human essentials to be lost sight of.

A theme running through my last lecture was that although in large social groupings such tendencies are inevitable, they can be none the less disastrous; that unless there are strong counteracting tendencies in the pre-political area there is always the danger that politics will breed not only abstract opinion but fanaticism and vio-lence. It is here, I suggested, that we see something of the importance of the artist when he deals with political or large-scale social situations: from the schematizations of propaganda and the simplifications of popular history he brings us back to the human and particular, and how-ever complex his material may be he holds it steadily in relation to fundamental values. My subject in this lecture however is not the artist and politics but some insights to be found in Shakespeare's political plays; and I shall say no more by way of introduction except this: that what Shakespeare teaches us in this respect is not anything that can be abstracted from the plays; it is available only in particular works of art, and available only to the extent that these are responded to individually, *as works of art*, with the whole force of our imaginations. Perhaps indeed to speak of his plays teaching us anything is misleading: they tell us nothing; they only prompt us to question, to feel, to think, and to see.

In the early political plays, *Henry VI* and *Richard III*, there is a marked formal quality. The events of history are shaped and patterned in order to focus clearly the operation of principles in particular sets of circumstances: there is indeed a certain stiffness and excess of formality as events are dramatized, not simply for the sake of the plot or the exhibition of interesting individuals, but to emphasize their representative character—as in the well-known stage directions, 'Enter a Son that has killed his father, dragging in the dead body', and 'Enter a Father that has killed his son, bringing in the body'.* In the later plays on political subjects we are clearly much nearer to the vitality and variety of life itself, but always there is a deliberate patterning of the plot—repetition, parallelism and contrast of situation and event—to focus whatever it is that lies at the heart of the drama. And besides the pattern of the action there is what we may pedantically call a pattern of attitudes of those engaged in the action: we notice the different ways of assessing or valuing the action that are brought into play, with *their* similarities, variations and contrasts. Those attitudes may be more or less explicit, as they are with Richard of Gloucester or, later, with Volumnia; or they may be implicit, as they are with most of the warring lords in *Richard III* or, later, with the taciturn Henry Bolingbroke. But whether explicit or merely implied they are not haphazard expressions of varied life-styles: they all relate to something at the centre of the action, whether we call it theme or organizing idea.

In reading Shakespeare's plays and trying to give some account of what we find there, we are, of course, continually reminded of the inadequacy of our critical terms, such as 'theme', 'character', or 'symbolic action': 'pattern' is no exception. The political plays *are* patterned in ways determined by an emergent theme or organizing interest; but we should be careful not to allow a descriptive term, with

---

* For the deliberate patterning of the *Henry VI* plays—'as stiff as the black and white squares on a chess-board'—see Hereward T. Price, 'Construction in Shakespeare' (University of Michigan, Contributions in Modern Philology), and the Introduction to *The First Part of King Henry VI* (New Arden Shakespeare), ed. Andrew S. Cairncross.

some limited and provisional use, to take over and save us from the continually renewed effort to see what is actually in front of us. Even at a superficial level what may seem to be an obvious pattern—as in the first tetralogy of history plays—is likely to be disturbed by elements that don't fit in—abrupt changes of the dramatic mode or shifts of perspective (like Clarence's dream or the occasional glimpses of Richard of Gloucester not as a development from the Vice of the morality plays but as a grown-up and brutally effective child delinquent).

The truth is, 'pattern' suggests simplification; whereas Shakespeare's patterning—if we call it that—is a device of compression that, in the greater plays, engages with and is inseparable from an almost overwhelming richness. Politics, we have noticed, tend to promote sweeping generalities. But Shakespeare, in the political plays, does not present generalized situations: there is nothing that can be more or less adequately summed up in a formula, such as 'the education of a patriot king', or—to quote Nahum Tate's title for his version of *Coriolanus*—'The Ingratitude of a Commonwealth'.* What he does give, in each play, is something sharply realized in human terms, a lively sense of a particular human situation with all its bothersome contradictions, and those untidy fringes of action that somehow refuse to be swept away as irrelevancies.

At this point we may invoke Erich Auerbach's phrase, 'perspective consciousness', which, he says, Shakespeare shares with the humanistic thought of his time. This is not only a sense of historical depth but an awareness of

---

* The moral, Tate said, was 'to Recommend Submission and Adherence to Establisht Lawful Power'. (Quoted by C. B. Young in his stage-history of the play in the New Cambridge edition, pp. xli-xlii.)

the varied possibilities of a multi-layered world.* And it is this perspective consciousness that largely determines the nature of the political plays, preventing them from becoming mere dramatizations of history or the embodiment of some preconceived idea. With few exceptions Shakespeare's political characters bring their world with them; and it is not easy to schematize a world. Again and again scenes or episodes are enacted or reported that, if they do nothing else, prevent us from seeing the political action as clearly silhouetted against a void. In fact of course they do more than that: they force us to make connexions between the apparently clear-cut alternatives of public action and the stubborn life of every-day, whether of noble or commoner. The wife of a murdered statesman tells of the desolation of her house:

> Alack, and what shall good old York there see
> But empty lodgings and unfurnished walls,
> Unpeopled offices, untrodden stones?

Power for a few is won or lost in battles, but the anonymous dead have not even the consolation of 'honour':

> And as the soldiers bore dead bodies by
> He call'd them untaught knaves, unmannerly,
> To bring a slovenly unhandsome corpse
> Betwixt the wind and his nobility.

The first thing we hear after Hotspur's enthusiasm for revolt ('O! let the hours be short, / Till fields and blows and groans applaud our sport!') is the yawn of a sleepy carrier, who glances at the stars to tell the time:

> Heigh-ho! An't be not four by the day I'll be hanged!
> Charles' wain is over the new chimney, and yet our
> horse not packed. What, ostler!

* Erich Auerbach, *Mimesis: the Representation of Reality in Western Literature*, 13, 'The Weary Prince'.

Readers of Shakespeare will hardly need to be reminded of the part played in the total action of *Henry IV*, Part II, by the evocation of life on a Gloucestershire manor, where the well-chain must be mended and the headland sown with red wheat, and where Mouldy's old mother will have no one to do 'her husbandry and her drudgery' if he goes off to the wars. Sometimes the opening up into a larger life is simply an effect of imagery and allusion; for as Coleridge said, 'Shakespeare always by metaphors and figures involves in the thing considered a universe of past and possible experiences'.*

> I had rather be a kitten and cry 'mew'
> Than one of these same metre ballad-mongers;
> I had rather hear a brazen canstick turn'd,
> Or a dry wheel grate on the axle-tree;
> And that would set my teeth nothing on edge,
> Nothing so much as mincing poetry;
> 'Tis like the forc'd gait of a shuffling nag
>   . . . . O! he's as tedious
> As a tired horse, a railing wife;
> Worse than a smoky house. I had rather live
> With cheese and garlick in a windmill, far,
> Than feed on cates and have him talk to me
> In any summer-house in Christendom.

Kittens, ballad-hawkers, candlestick-makers, the ungreased wheels of farm-carts, draughty windmills . . . these are all parts of the life of common humanity, which the nobles may ignore in their strategic planning, but we, their spectators, cannot.†

What we cannot ignore—what, more positively, we are alerted to—is largely determined by Shakespeare's use of

* Coleridge, *Lectures and Notes on Shakespeare and Other English Poets*, ed. T. Ashe (Bohn's Popular Library), p. 406.

† Professor A. R. Humphreys, in his Introduction to the New Arden edition of *I Henry IV*, rightly speaks of the play's 'rich embedding in social life. . . This swarming social and national life is set in place and time.'

language. I have spoken of the obtrusive patterning of the action in the early political plays, which is matched by the formal rhetorical patterning of so many of the speeches.* But in addition to dramatic stylization of this kind, there is also, almost from the start, another element, represented by a strain of colloquial and idiomatic speech which, even in the early plays, contrasts with, and to some extent undercuts the formal rhetoric. And the importance of 'the diction of common-life'†—the common, forthright, non-literary idiom of, for example, the Bastard in *King John*—is that through it we see things directly for what they are, with a consequent deflation of convention, whether literary, social or political. In other words, the colloquial style is the verbal equivalent of a moral habit of seeing the naked human actuality which, in the world of political and social antagonisms, is so often obscured. I have used before a passage from the Shakespearian pages of the play *Sir Thomas More*, which is apt to my present purpose. More, as Sheriff, is trying to persuade a crowd of London citizens to stop their riot against alien immigrants:

> Grant them removed, and grant that this your noise
> Hath chid down all the majesty of England!
> Imagine that you see the wretched strangers,
> Their babies at their backs, with their poor luggage,
> Plodding to the ports and coasts for transportation. . . .

My comment was to the effect that in those lines the generic concept 'aliens'—so useful for demagogic appeals —is replaced by the specifically rendered 'strangers'; that the generalized abstractions of propaganda give way to the actual and particular. And this, I claimed, is Shake-

* See A. P. Rossiter, 'The Unity of Richard III', in *Angel with Horns.*

† See F. P. Wilson, 'Shakespeare and the Diction of Common Life' in *'Shakespearian and Other Studies'* (ed. Helen Gardner) and Hilda Hulme, *Explorations in Shakespeare's Language.*

speare's characteristic way of dealing with political and social situations that lend themselves only too easily to the process of simplification by which notions and ideas take the place of the complexities of the actual.* In *King Lear* we are not invited to 'consider the problem of poverty': we are invited to make vividly present to our imagination what it feels like to be homeless, starving and half-naked. So too, although the nature of justice is a constant preoccupation in this play, the meanings that, under Shakespeare's guidance, we form for ourselves come from the interaction of vivid particular presentations that compel a strong working of the mind.

> . . . see how yond justice rails upon yon simple thief. Hark, in thine ear: change places; and, handy-dandy, which is the justice, which is the thief, Thou hast seen a farmer's dog bark at a beggar? . . . And the creature run from the cur? There thou mightst behold the great image of authority; a dog's obey'd in office.

Perspective consciousness, then, is not simply a matter of opening up and filling in something we can safely think of as 'background'; it is a steady reminder that what political and social questions are, ultimately, about, is the ways in which one person or group of persons affects another person or group of persons. And just as the effects of political action can only be felt by some individual consciousness ('My paths, my walks, my manors that I had / Even now forsake me'), so the causes are to be sought in the inter-action of persons and—a point to which we shall return—the recesses of the individual personality; for there is an opening of inner perspective as well as perspectives on the social scene.

* L. C. Knights, 'Poetry, Politics and the English Tradition', in *Further Explorations*. See also, in the same volume, 'Shakespeare's Politics' and 'The Personalism of Julius Caesar'.

The result of course is that in the political plays, where we are forced by the very nature of the dramatic method to ponder the rights and wrongs of the public issues at stake, those issues are presented in all their complexity. In *Richard II* the balance of sympathy and antipathy as between Richard and Bolingbroke not only determines the main structural lines of the play, it permeates particular scenes in minutest detail.* It is because of the pervasive pressure of the actual that we are compelled to judge, and that we find judgment so difficult. As A. C. Bradley said: '[Shakespeare's] impartiality makes us uncomfortable. . . . And this is perhaps especially the case in his history plays, where we are always trying to turn him into a partisan. He shows us that Richard II was unworthy to be king, and we at once conclude that he thought Bolingbroke's usurpation justified; whereas he shows merely, what under the conditions was bound to exist, an inextricable tangle of right and unright.'† What he reflects for us, in short, is a world where those schematized abstractions that guarantee our political righteousness have no place.

Professor Norman Rabkin has remarked that 'there is only one constant in Shakespeare's political plays: the view of politics as problematic'.‡ This, though not often commented on, could hardly be otherwise, in view of the problematic nature of most human relationships and antagonisms, of which political relationships and antagonisms form a part. In *Felix Holt* George Eliot reminds us

* See Brents Stirling, *Unity in Shakespearean Tragedy*, Chapter 3, and Ernest William Talbert, *The Problem of Order: Elizabethan Political Commonplace and an Example of Shakespeare's Art*, Chapter 6.

† A. C. Bradley, 'The Rejection of Falstaff', *Oxford Lectures on Poetry*, p. 255.

‡ Norman Rabkin, *Shakespeare and the Common Understanding*, p. 81. In *Shakespeare's Political Plays* Professor M. M. Richmond similarly speaks of Shakespeare as 'politically alert, yet sceptical of facile solutions', and refers to the 'complex political tensions' that run through *Richard II*.

that 'there is no private life which has not been determined by a wider public life'. The statement could, I think, be reversed: at all events, when we turn our attention from directly personal to public affairs, we should not be so bedevilled by the word 'public' as to forget all that we are aware of in reading Jane Austen, George Eliot or Henry James—or, for that matter, in our own lives.

Think for a moment of the large and dismal subject of quarrels and misunderstandings. Any observer of human nature, his own included, must have been struck by the similarities between some forms of political debate and the common quarrel. Most quarrels—not all, for some, as Coleridge observed, are merely a way of passing the time, like spitting over bridges—have a hard core of disagreement about some particular issue and the proper way of handling it. Where disagreement occurs the purpose of rational discussion would be to define the object in dispute—to establish the facts, so far as they can be established—and to clarify the principles or assumptions applied by the participants, with a view to achieving as much agreement as possible. When disagreements become quarrels something quite different happens. Facts are distorted or concealed by emotions drawn from a wide range of resentments, projections, aggressions, thwarted desires, and so on, with the result that the particular matter at issue becomes little more than a badly lighted area for the conflict of forces that have as it were smuggled themselves in. Quarrels are bad not simply because they involve hatred but because they obfuscate the understanding. We may note here for later use the related phenomenon of not listening—not really listening to the person you are ostensibly speaking to—that unfortunately governs so much of the field of human relationships, and that is brilliantly satirized by Blake in *An Island in the Moon*.

Now Shakespeare is good at presenting scenes of quarrel and dispute: think, for example, of the quarrel between Brutus and Cassius in *Julius Caesar*, Act IV, scene ii. One way into the play of *Richard II* is to see what we can learn from the scenes of quarrel, mutual recrimination and defiance that occur at the beginning and in the middle of the play (I, i and IV, i). Since the play is carefully constructed to show the opposition and contrast of two political types, one rising as the other falls, the second half of the play, with Bolingbroke in the ascendant, may be expected to throw some retrospective light on the first half. Act IV, scene i, shows Bolingbroke exercising kingly power before he is actually king. Like Richard at the opening of the play he hears a dispute about what went on 'in that dead time when Gloucester's death was plotted'. (What time, the play makes us ask, is ever dead?) As we should expect, he is more efficient and decisive than Richard was in roughly similar circumstances, when Bolingbroke and Mowbray were the disputants. But there is not only contrast, there is reinforcement. Consider briefly how the action goes. Bagot, a royal favourite who is now trying to ingratiate himself with Bolingbroke, accuses Aumerle, Richard's cousin and friend, of causing Gloucester's death, as well as arguing against Bolingbroke's recall from banishment. Bagot is joined by Percy, Fitzwater and another Lord. At a climactic moment Surrey—who is admitted to have been present when Aumerle allegedly spoke the incriminating words—comes to Aumerle's defence. The stage is littered with gloves thrown down in challenge, but that doesn't help us at all in trying to determine which side is right. The votes are four to two (of whom one is Aumerle himself), but that is not necessarily conclusive, since we notice a good deal that tells against Aumerle's accusers, such as Fitzwater's asseveration, 'As I intend to thrive in this new world'.[7] But in this emotionally charged atmosphere it is impossible to get at the truth about Gloucester's death, and in this respect the scene is a diminished echo of the confused charges and counter-charges that we heard at the beginning of the play. That first scene not only establishes the Richard/Bolingbroke opposition, it not only alerts us to qualities in the King that will be more fully displayed when Richard is not acting a public part, it tells us a good deal about the obfuscations of public life when heady declamation is the only outlet for hidden interests and emotions—hidden, sometimes, even from the agent himself. These are not of course simply quarrels in the street. Also involved are reasons of state, with their fathomless abysses*; and the need not to bring these fully into the open, the sense that the protagonists cannot, or dare not, admit them fully even to themselves, contributes powerfully to what Dr Sanders has called the play's 'moral obscurity'—'an opacity in the texture of the drama which has been deliberately cultivated'.† The quarrels are part of the manœuvring of political antagonists; that is to say, they are about power in the state and not about the pecking-order in a small social group. But 'big' quarrels are part of a series that includes 'little' quarrels, and the differences introduced by the size of the interests involved, or their life-and-death quality, should not obscure the real similarities. When political activity seems to move in a sphere remote from that of every-day, it simply admits its all too human weaknesses by a back door and gives them other names.

Not listening is another matter that makes its negative

* 'That fathomless abyss of reason of state'—Clarendon.
† Wilbur Sanders, *The Dramatist and the Received Idea*, Chapter xi—a very perceptive account, which faces the play's perplexities with great honesty.

contribution to politics as it does to domestic, social or academic life. A minor, but significant, example is the opening of the first scene of Act II in *Coriolanus* where Menenius uses his far from impartial urbanity and his reputation for whimsicality to exasperate the Tribunes, whom he rightly expects to be dismayed by the personal triumph of Caius Marcius over the Volsces. It would be easy to go through the episode in detail to show how question and answer, statement and counter-statement, fail to engage in any significant interchange. Verbal side-stepping, truths mixed with partial truths and untruths, abuse disguised as wit (so that the abused has no defence), straightforward abuse that may or may not be deserved,[8] all prevent any serious coming to terms with what, after all, is the main point at issue—whether or not Marcius is 'proud', and whether, or to what extent, this disqualifies him from civic office. There is a good deal of play on the verb 'to know', but what the scene brings out is that neither side knows the other in any full and direct sense. Menenius's reply to Brutus's feeble, 'Come, sir, come, we know you well enough'—'You know neither me, your-selves, nor any thing', might be retorted on himself; and his vulgar abuse of the Tribunes serves to underline the mutual incomprehension of both sides. When Volumnia, Virgilia and Valeria enter and the Tribunes stand aside, Menenius's marked change of manner

> —How now, my as fair as noble ladies, and the moon, were she earthly, no nobler, whither do you follow your eyes so fast?—

shows the patricians withdrawing into the closed circle of their caste, with its fixed and limiting assumptions. *Coriolanus* is, among other things, a study of the barriers to communication in the state, the so-called body politic, which gives the lie to Menenius's disingenuous fable of the belly; it is about a failure of relationship which can be disastrous both for individuals and for the state at large.[9]

Before I try to sum up these scattered observations there is a further point, already touched on, that needs to be made explicit. John Palmer, at the end of an excellent chapter on *Coriolanus*, says, 'The politics are . . . in the last analysis incidental. Shakespeare is intent on persons, not on public affairs.'* But this is an over-sharp distinction. In Shakespeare's political plays—not least in *Coriolanus*†—politics are shown as an affair of persons. Erich Auerbach, whose term 'perspective consciousness' I have appropriated, says of Montaigne,

> in his study of his own random life Montaigne's sole aim is an investigation of the *humaine condition* in general; and with that he reveals the heuristic principle which we constantly employ . . . when we endeavour to understand and judge the acts of others, whether the acts of our close associates or more remote acts which belong in the realms of politics or history. We apply criteria to them which we have derived from our own lives and our own inner experience—so that our knowledge of men and of history depends upon the depth of our own self-knowledge and the extent of our moral horizon.‡

In Shakespeare, when great public events are involved, there is an opening of inner, as well as of social, perspectives, and we are never allowed to forget that the two are inextricably related. This is more than a matter of the psychology of the characters: Shakespeare only shows us as much of that as serves his purpose, but what he does reveal is central to the political action.

* John Palmer, *The Political Characters of Shakespeare*, pp. 308-9.

† In *Some Shakespearean Themes*, Chapter vii, I sketched my own view of the way in which Coriolanus' partial failure in the field of politics is related to his failure to grow up, his failure—under his mother's influence—as a man.

‡ *Mimesis*, pp. 301-2.

That he intends us to make the connexion is plain
enough from the way in which 'public' and 'private'
scenes are juxtaposed, the way in which public roles are
made transparent to the concealed life behind them. We
may return briefly to *Richard II*, that splendid study of
a weak, vain, egotistical self-deceiver who is called to
play the part of a king, who so wretchedly fails, and who,
in failing, learns things about himself that he had not
known in prosperity. The structure of the first Act is
simple but significant. Scene i gives the public surface—a
quarrel of two powerful lords, with the partial exercise
of kingly power. Scene ii reminds us of the underside of
public life: on the one hand the connivance of the king
in the murder of Gloucester, on the other the private
misery caused by dynastic feuds. Scene iii, in the lists at
Coventry, is again a public scene: Richard, in stopping
the judicial combat and banishing both Mowbray and
Bolingbroke, exercises the authority of a king; but we
are beginning to feel some doubts about the moral bases
of that authority. Scene iv, the last of the Act, is a close-
up: Richard is seen with his confidential advisers, and
again, in his heartlessness and his cynical swerving from
justice, we have a glimpse of the underside, of what is
hidden from the public view.[10] In sum, Act I not only
prepares us for the Richard/Bolingbroke contrast that
will be worked out later, it prompts some questions:
What are the realities beneath Richard's formal and
ceremonious public world? What sort of a man is it that
makes this dubious impression?

It is easy to sentimentalize Richard, to respond only to
the pathos that he spreads around him; but Shakespeare
doesn't sentimentalize him. Here he is on his return from
his Irish expedition, when Bolingbroke is already march-
ing against him.

> I weep for joy
> To stand upon my kingdom once again.
> Dear earth, I do salute thee with my hand,
> Though rebels wound thee with their horses' hoofs:
> As a long parted mother with her child
> Plays fondly with her tears and smiles in meeting,
> So, weeping, smiling, greet I thee, my earth,
> And do thee favours with my royal hands.

All very touching, but unfortunately with no relation at
all to reality. Has Richard been in any sense a mother
to his land? When we last saw him he had been engaged
in unjust and arbitrary financial extortion; and our
memory of that not only makes his claim to be a parent
to his country into another characteristic bit of senti-
mental make-believe, it throws a very critical light on
the claim to divine right that Richard goes on to make.
Shakespeare knew that kings and rulers had responsi-
bilities to something greater than themselves, and although Richard makes a pretty picture out of his pleasure
at being again on English soil—'So, weeping, smiling,
greet I thee, my earth'—the little phrase 'my earth'
contains a quite outrageous claim; and the play makes
us know it. Richard, it is true, slowly and painfully approaches sincerity and self-knowledge,

> Nay, if I turn mine eyes upon myself,
> I find myself a traitor with the rest . . .

> I wasted time, and now doth time waste me . . .,

—but in the passage I have just read he is very far indeed
from sincerity and common sense. When, as Shakespeare
asks you to do, you make connexions, put two and two
together, you find that the play is a study of the meaning
of sincerity, and of the relation between personal integrity,
or the lack of it, and events in the public world. We can

put this another way. In *Richard II* the achievement of sincerity, of at least some degree of self-knowledge, is seen as a painful impeded movement of the whole personality. That is the central psychological interest of the play. But in our present context it has a further relevance. Just as what comes to a focus in the individual consciousness has behind it a network of pressures, some only partly conscious, so in the political and public realm what takes place and can be recorded in history is the manifestation of what is prepared in the inner lives of men and in the network of individual relations that constitute a political society. That, incidentally, is why Shakespeare shows that there is no easy solution to the political problem.

Compared with Shakespeare most of the contemporary dramatists, when they deal with political issues or touch on politics, appear as simplifiers. A full survey would, I suppose, include Massinger, with the 'rank republicanism' that has been imputed to him, and Beaumont and Fletcher, with their '*jure divino* principles . . . carried to excess'.* More important, there is Chapman, for whose power as a political thinker serious claims have been made.[11] But there is a greater dramatist than any of these —Ben Jonson; and I hope his ghost will forgive me if I refer briefly to *Sejanus* in order to emphasize some of the things I have been trying to say about Shakespeare.

Sejanus still seems to me, as it seemed thirty-five years ago, a great and unjustly neglected play.† Jonson of course got his material from classical sources, and his standards derive in part from his reading in the Latin classics. But just as the historical material is transmuted

---

* Coleridge, *Shakespearean Criticism*, ed. T. M. Raysor (Everyman edn.), Vol. I, p. 122. Compare: 'Massinger is a decided Whig;—Beaumont and Fletcher high-flying, passive-obedience, Tories'.—*Lectures on Shakespeare*, ed. T. Ashe (Bohn's Popular Library), p. 437.

† I refer to my *Drama and Society in the Age of Jonson* (1937), Chapter vi.

by being passed through Jonson's own mind, so his admiration for the old Roman republican virtues is related to, is part of, his liveliest feelings about the present in which he lived. In other words the political positives of the play—whether implied or directly expressed through his choric figures—are an expression of that independence of mind and dislike of subservience that we find in his poems, and the play as a whole is a powerful and dramatically effective comment on some permanent features of political life.

But *Sejanus* is a play of which the greatness depends on severe limitations. It is 'moralized history' in massively simple terms, as you see in the sharp distinction between the good characters—Arruntius, Silius, Sabinus—and the evil ones—Tiberius, Sejanus, Livia, Macro and the time-serving senators: there is no shading.* Jonson defines by exaggeration and caricature a form of evil that can destroy a state. But even apart from his failure to endow with much genuine life the characters who speak out for such positive values as the play contains, the method of presentation must ultimately hinder our understanding of the moral bases of politics. The play relies very heavily indeed on moral generalities, the 'fulness and frequence of sentence' that Jonson prides himself on in the Address to the Reader—such as the lines that were prudently altered in the Folio,

> all best Turns
> With Princes, do convert to injuries,

—to which it is almost too easy to assent. Jonson's world is not, like Shakespeare's, a world of many-faceted

---

* He clearly found congenial his principal source, the *Annals* of Tacitus. Tacitus' view of history as exhibiting a fairly clear-cut opposition between good and evil is discussed by Michael Grant in the Introduction to his translation of the *Annals of Imperial Rome* (Penguin Classics).

relationships, it is a world of figures who manipulate each other, from the outside.[12] In presenting a situation in which all shadings of right and wrong are ignored, Jonson offers an *exemplum* that can only be applied to the most extreme situations. Whereas Shakespeare in *Richard II* forces the recognition of complexity, Jonson encourages a black-and-white view of political situations in general, and the suspicion emerges that even he may have had some share in encouraging the simplifiers who were to disrupt English society in the seventeenth century. He certainly encourages the view that evil is *outside you*, something to be scornfully attacked. You can't apply to his tragedies, as you can to Shakespeare's, Yeats's remark that in great tragedy 'it is always ourselves that we see upon the stage'.*

Since Shakespeare and Ben Jonson are both, in their very different ways, very much alive, to establish differences of degree of 'greatness' between them is a barren exercise, and I must emphasize again that I am only doing so for the particular purpose I have in hand. What we come back to is the question of language, of the way in which the poet uses words, which in turn determines the nature of the world presented to our imagination, and the ways in which we respond to that world. Professor Christopher Ricks has shown that in *Sejanus* there is a strong underlying drive towards disruption.† But it is not what one may call creative disruption. Jonson brilliantly lives up to his own maxim: 'The chief virtue of a style is perspicuity, and nothing so vicious in it as to need an interpreter'. But his hard clarity ignores whatever may be going on underneath, ignores in fact that there

* W. B. Yeats, 'The Tragic Theatre' (originally published in *The Cutting of an Agate*), *Essays and Introductions*, p. 241.

† Christopher Ricks, '*Sejanus* and Dismemberment', *Modern Language Notes*, 76, 1961, pp. 301-8.

may be an underneath: it does not open up the springs of confusion and chaos so that we can understand and so, perhaps, control them. In Shakespeare's political plays, on the other hand, not only are the situations problematic—especially so in the opening of each play— the key terms are problematic too, and they are broken down to reveal the human complexities and distortions that lie behind their apparent simplicity. Think, for example, of the ways in which, in *Coriolanus*, we are forced to examine the criss-cross of unspoken assumptions that lie behind such words as 'the state', 'honour', 'obedience', 'flattery' and 'valour'. And the clash of meanings behind the words reflects the intricate tangle of relationships and misunderstandings which underlies the more overt forms of conflict.[13]

Shakespeare, I have tried to show, is—if we define our terms properly—a political thinker of the first order. When we refer to 'political thought' we normally and properly have in mind such works as, say, Machiavelli's *The Prince* or Hobbes's *Leviathan*—the work of men who at least attempt more or less dispassionately to elicit general laws of political behaviour. Such studies can never, of course, be strictly scientific, but in some important ways they look towards science. Stuart Hampshire, for example, praises Spinoza because in his conception of society he anticipated 'a modern, *scientific* approach to sociology and politics'; he attempted to understand society '*objectively* as a balance of forces' (my italics).*
Now the attempt to understand society 'objectively', to reach understanding at a high level of generality, is of course necessary. My point is that, even with the needs of political thinking in mind, Shakespeare is doing something

* Stuart Hampshire, *Spinoza* (Pelican Philosophy Series, 1951), p. 189.

equally necessary, even though it is so obviously different from what Machiavelli or Hobbes or Spinoza in the *Tractatus Theologico-Politicus* or (to take an example of a different kind) Crane Brinton in *The Anatomy of Revolution*, are attempting to do.* I can perhaps sharpen the distinction with the help of some remarks made by Erik Erikson in his essay, 'Psychological Reality and Historical Actuality',† where he attempts a distinction between the two terms, 'reality' and 'actuality'. 'Reality' is 'the world of things really existing in the outer world'. But besides the 'outer' world—the world of the objectively real, which we can describe and measure—there is the world in which we actively and intuitively *participate*, for which we may use the word 'actuality', with its connotations of presentness and immediacy. It is the distinction suggested here that we need when we consider the differences between one of Shakespeare's greater political plays—say, *Coriolanus*—and the work of thinkers who consider political behaviour objectively and dispassionately, as exhibiting certain recurrences that allow the formulation of generalizations or—if we don't press the word too hard—'laws'. Obviously the treatises of the political philosophers and social-political investigators can offer insights that are genuine aids to understanding; yet perhaps at the cost of a certain thinning out of the rich diversity that forms their starting-point. Using Erikson's terms, we can say that they give a generalized account of external 'reality' as objectively as possible. What Shakespeare gives in *Coriolanus* is the 'actuality' of a political situation, and in it 'studies of "outer" conditions and of

* In an inaugural lecture, 'The Study of History and Political Science Today' published in *Theoria* (University of Natal Press), Vol. XXVI, June 1966, Professor Mark Prestwich makes some suggestive distinctions between political philosophy, political theory, and political thought.

† In his book, *Insight and Responsibility*.

"inner" states meet in one focus'. The political world that Shakespeare presents, in different plays, is a world not only of interacting forces but of 'participation' and 'mutual activation', or of the tragic lack of these qualities; and in presenting it as such Shakespeare restores a necessary dimension to political thinking.*

It is because of Shakespeare's awareness of the problematic in politics, of the embedding of the political in the social, and of the fact, finally, that society, far from being an aggregation of individuals, is a network of interpersonal relationships—the person himself depending for his very sense of self on those myriad vibrations of liking, disliking, validation and challenge that extend almost indefinitely in all directions—it is because of Shakespeare's awareness of all this, conveyed in a language that is itself a part of the intricate state of affairs for which it compels recognition, that he is—or could be if properly read—a perennial source of political wisdom. He incites us to look beyond politics as commonly understood to 'that kind of politics which is inwoven with human nature'.† To put the matter at its simplest, he reminds us of what, in political action, men forget at the peril of giving themselves over to the abstractions that can triumph over life. He reminds us of the need to keep our communications open and, even in a world where we have to choose and to act, to subject our political thinking to the actualities of life as we know it.

---

* That 'individual experience is no more merely private than society is merely public', and that in Shakespeare the self and its world are shown as mutually involved, is the main theme of Terence Eagleton's *Shakespeare and Society.*

† Coleridge, *Shakespearean Criticism*, ed. Raysor (Everyman edn.), Vol. I, p. 122.

CHAPTER THREE

Hooker and Milton: A Contrast
of Styles

(i)

BOTH for the student of literature and for the student
of history the period that runs from Shakespeare to
Dryden is in many ways exemplary: by which I do not
mean that it offers only examples to be followed. Coleridge
had a way of referring to the period from the Reformation
to the Revolution of 1688, in all that concerned the 'influence of intellect, information, prevailing principles and
tendencies', as offering an entirely favourable contrast to
the age immediately preceding his own, dominated by
'the Mechanic philosophy'. The truth is not so simple.
The seventeenth century contained its own share of
bigotry, bloody-mindedness, and plain stupidity. Even
its great men had their blind-sides and sometimes argued
in the tone of narrow partisans. But it does seem true to
say that in the seventeenth century there was available
a language for talking about politics that had a moral and
imaginative resonance, that was capable of dealing with
complex issues in all their complexity and particularity,
whilst at the same time opening up wider perspectives.
And the existence of this language throws into sharper
relief the language of the simplifiers, whose devices of
style narrow rather than broaden the field of vision. The
distinction of course is not absolute: different and even
opposed qualities can be found in the same writer; the
gradations are virtually infinite; and virtue is not to be

found only on one side of a political—or religious—
division at any time. But the distinctions are there, and
to try to define them is to learn a good deal about the
fundamental contrast between a political language that
is 'open'—looking towards the more-than-political, whatever the convictions of its speaker—and one that is
'closed', that in a greater or lesser degree attempts to
dominate and control the listener or reader.

In my last lecture I tried to suggest how Shakespeare
could enlarge and invigorate our thinking about politics.
There is a similar largeness of view, an opening up of
perspectives, in the work of Shakespeare's great contemporary, Richard Hooker. Where the differences are
so obvious—between the 'uncommitted' dramatist on the
one hand and the apologist for the Elizabethan Church
establishment on the other—there is no need to insist on
them. I am invoking Hooker here because his contribution to the climate of opinion in which political as well as
ecclesiastical issues could be discussed is something which,
like that of Shakespeare's plays, is no less important for
being elusive and incapable of exact formulation. What is
in question is not a specific doctrine but the attitudes that
lie behind doctrine, a preparation of the minds of men
to look at great public questions in a way that is open,
flexible and implicitly *connective*, rather than blinkered,
rigid, and narrowly partisan. He is of course a great
exponent of reason—which means that he believed in
certain universal standards and laws. But as Mr Christopher Morris remarks in his classic survey, *Political
Thought in England: Tyndale to Hooker*, 'Hooker feared
logical extremes and over-simple generalizations. "General rules", he said, "are, by reason of the manifold
secret exceptions which lie hidden in them, no other to
the eye of man's understanding than cloudy mists cast

before the eye of commonsense. . . . With gross and popular capacities nothing doth more prevail than unlimited generalities, because of their plainness at the first sight: nothing less with men of exact judgment." Much of Hooker's objection to the Puritans was due to their contempt for compromise and to their insistence on allowing no exceptions.'[14]

Hooker's most direct contribution to political thought is in Book VIII of *The Laws of Ecclesiastical Polity*, which 'sets forth the theory of a limited and constitutional monarchy, with the Crown subject to the law and with the seat of sovereignty resting in the people'. The modern editor of Book VIII, Aaron Houk, whom I have just quoted,* believes that Book VIII was not published in the 1590s, when it was written, simply because it was too radical for the times. On the other hand, it may well have been put out in 1648 (the date of first publication) because of its constitutionalism, as 'part of a campaign to win the King back to a more moderate view of the royal prerogative and the people to a reasonable allegiance to the King'.† This view—like Houk's further claims that the *Polity* as a whole is 'a brilliant treatise on the true nature of the English state', that Book VIII spells out what is implicit in Book I, 'Concerning Laws and their Several Kinds', and that 'there is little in modern democratic theory which cannot be found in Hooker's First Book'—is a matter for specialists. Why Hooker is important for non-specialists can be summed up under three heads: (*a*) the grounds of his objections to radical puritanism; (*b*) the nature of his general thought about man in

* Hooker's *Ecclesiastical Polity*, Book VIII, with an Introduction by Raymond Aaron Houk (Columbia University Press, 1931), Introduction, p. 6.

† *Op. cit.*, p. 117. Cf. p. 145: the Book was published 'probably to provide the Parliamentarians and the King with a theory of a limited monarchy by which a reconciliation might be effected'.

society; and (c) his style and manner. I can only touch on each of these very briefly indeed, in an attempt to bring out what lies behind the defence of the Elizabethan Church settlement that can be used in very different circumstances, when we think of permanent questions concerning stability and innovation, permanence and progression, or the difficult balance between moderation and a willingness to accept radical change.

Hooker's account of the Calvinistic discipline, of the reasons for its appeal, and of the dangers of the Puritan movement, form the substance of his Preface. This is worth attention from others than historians because much of what Hooker says might well be applied to many forms of oversimplifying 'revolutionary' propaganda, secular as well as religious. He notes in particular: the tendency to attribute all faults, including those common to human nature as such, to the established order of things ('He that goes about to persuade a multitude, that they are not so well governed as they ought to be, shall never want attentive and favourable hearers' (Book I, i, 67)); the tendency to believe that what is least tried is likeliest to bring improvement; and, perhaps most important of all, the fact that the strength of the puritan appeal lay in its apparent simplification of complex issues. If everything necessary is contained in The Book, you can with a good conscience make a clean sweep of history and tradition.[15] Behind such attitudes lurks the notion of perfectibility that was later to find expression in millenarianism and in various forms of secular thought. We may call to mind both Coleridge's analysis of Jacobinism ('legislative geometry') in *The Friend* and Arnold's warning about the dangers of Hebraizing in *Culture and Anarchy*.

To Puritan individualism—its over-emphasis on private judgment—Hooker opposes a sense of the necessarily cooperative nature of the human enterprise both in the religious and the secular sphere. He is Aristotelian and medieval in his insistence on man's need for society: the state is necessary not just negatively as a bulwark against a 'natural' predatoriness (as in the Hobbesian myth), but positively, to help towards full human development—'a life fit for the dignity of man'. Of the two foundations 'which bear up human societies', the first is 'a natural inclination whereby all men desire sociable life and fellowship'.* There is, he says,

> a natural delight which man hath to transfuse from himself into others, and to receive from others into himself especially those things wherein the excellency of his kind doth most consist. The chiefest instrument of human communication therefore is speech, because thereby we impart mutually one to another the conceits of our mutual understanding. . . . Civil society doth more content the nature of man than any private kind of solitary living, because in society this good of mutual participation is so much larger than otherwise. Herein notwithstanding we are not satisfied, but we covet (if it might be) to have a kind of society and fellowship even with all mankind (I, x, 12).

Civilization is, therefore, so far as possible, a matter of mutuality and cooperation; and it involves cooperation not only between the living, but between the living and the dead.

> We die with the dying:
> See, they depart, and we go with them.
> We are born with the dead:
> See they return, and bring us with them.

The past is alive in us; but the forms of civilization are not immutable. As Professor d'Entrèves has pointed

* The second, deriving from the first, is 'an order expressly or secretly agreed upon touching the manner of their union in living together' (I, x, i).

out, 'the laws of ecclesiastical—and *a fortiori* of civil—polity, are removed from the control of a rigid appeal to the Bible and conceived in terms of historical convenience and development'.[16] 'Some kinds of regiment,' says Hooker, 'the Law of Nature doth require; yet the kinds thereof being many, Nature tieth not to one, but leaveth the choice as a thing arbitrary' (I, x, 5). Remarks such as this remind us that Hooker not only looks back to the Christian and classical tradition, but forward to later developments in political thought. He is a great channel of communication, through which, as Mr Morris says, 'the voice of medieval Catholic philosophy could make itself heard to the coming generation of Protestant Whigs, to such men as Locke and Algernon Sidney'.*

It has been necessary to touch on these matters, however briefly and inadequately, to bring out what I most want to say about Hooker. The point is put by Edmund Dowden (in *Puritan and Anglican*): 'Important as may be the results arrived at by Hooker's argument, his method and temper are more important. His influence is at once to liberalize and to sober the mind of one who has submitted to his teaching.' It is 'his method and temper' that I want to call attention to. The manner and style—the manner and style of reasonableness and courtesy—are in themselves a contribution to the health of political thinking. He could of course be tart:

> By these and the like disputes an opinion hath spread itself very far in the world, as if the way to be ripe in faith were to be raw in wit and judgment (III, viii, 4).

Or,

> Few there be of so weak capacity, but public evils they easily espy (V, i, 1).

* *Op. cit*, pp. 196-7. See also Charles Mills Gayley, *Shakespeare and the Founders of Liberty in America*, Chapter v, 'Richard Hooker, and the Principles of American Liberty'.

Or,

> To seek reformation of evil laws is a commendable endeavour;
> but for us the more necessary is a speedy redress of ourselves
> (V, Dedication, 2).

But the prevailing tone is that of a reasonable persuader, not that of a controversialist*; it is the tone of a man who believes that 'the bounds of wisdom are large, and within them much is contained' (II, i, 4). 'Be it that Cephas hath one interpretation, and Apollos hath another; that Paul is of this mind and Barnabas of that; if this offend you, the fault is yours. *Carry peaceable minds, and ye may have comfort by this variety.*'†

That, of course, is a counsel of perfection. Variety is not always so easily accommodated: it may show itself as a tragic clash of opposites. But what essentially Hooker is pleading for is the diminution of a self-righteous intolerance, based on fear and self-mistrust: for as Jeremy Taylor was to say later, all the manifestations of intolerance, whether the persecution of men or of books 'show that we either distrust God for the maintenance of his truth, or that we distrust the cause, or distrust ourselves and our abilities'.‡ To admire this—as I do—is not to refuse to recognize the need for a strong assertion of one's own values, even when they are radically opposed to those of others, even when the others form a majority:

---

* Cf., 'Wherein our endeavour is not so much to overthrow them with whom we contend, as to yield them just and reasonable causes of those things, which for want of due consideration heretofore, they misconceived' (V, i, 1).

† 'A Learned Discourse of Justification',—Everyman edn. of *The Laws of Ecclesiastical Polity*, Vol. I, p. 75.

‡ Jeremy Taylor, Epistle Dedicatory to *A Discourse of the Liberty of Prophesying, Whole Works* (1880), p. 300. 'For it is a hard case that we should think all papists, and anabaptists, and sacramentaries, to be fools and wicked persons: certainly, among all these sects, there are very many wise men and good men, as well as erring.'—*Op. cit.*, p. 294.

Blake was not noted for an easy compliance with prevailing opinion. But without the presence somewhere in one's mind, somewhere in the mind of an age, of Hooker's tolerance and openness, necessary assertion of one's values can degenerate into something that undercuts the values for which one professes to stand.

A blend of firm conviction and tolerant openness is not easy to maintain in any age. In the seventeenth century there were many reasons why good men should find themselves radically opposed—opposed, even, to the death; and it would be a paltry kind of detachment that regarded the clash of the civil war as based on nothing but bigotry and misunderstanding. But when we turn to that war and what succeeded it, it is, all the same, necessary and useful for us to see how the political language even of 'committed' men appears when measured against standards which both Shakespeare and Hooker, in their different ways, incite us to make our own.

(ii)

In the remainder of this lecture, and in the following one, I wish to look at certain writings that were products of the great conflict of arms and ideas that has been called variously the Rebellion, the Civil War, or the English Revolution. Although the causes and nature of that conflict are still being debated by historians, it is necessary to say something about it before looking at the texts that will be the main objects of attention. Since the abandonment of the over-simplified 'Whig' view—that the Civil War and its aftermath showed a fairly straightforward movement towards the establishment of English political and religious liberty—causes have been sought in the particular interests of particular sections of the community, especially the economic interests. For example, the war was the attempt of increasingly powerful classes —the mercantile and trading classes, and the rising gentry with whom they were allied—to burst through outmoded constitutional forms that favoured the King and the old aristocracy. Unfortunately this too is an oversimplification: not all the monied men opposed the King, and not all the great nobles supported him. Nor is it possible to invoke some such formula as 'the rise of the gentry'—a class which, according to Professor Trevor-Roper, was depressed rather than rising. And even if Trevor-Roper is right that 'in the 1630s, incidental political factors increased this depression, and the radical gentry willingly supported the aristocratic politicians who sought, by parliamentary pressure, to bring the King back into the ancient constitutional ways',* the picture is further complicated by the fact that in many parts of the country what side a man was on was determined as much by local interests as by involvement in national issues, and that many men, on both sides, were genuinely actuated by religious motives: when we survey the past ideals cannot always be subsumed into ideology. A well-known passage in Marvell's *The Rehearsal Transprosed* (1672) warns us against looking for any massively simple explanation: 'Whether it be a war of religion or of liberty, is not worth the labour to enquire. Whichsoever was at the top, the other was at the bottom.' All that is clear is that in the years 1640 to 1660 there was a complex clash of interests and ideals that can be traced back at least as far as the closing years of the reign of Elizabeth I. Professor Zagorin, in *The Court and the Country*, produces a

* H. R. Trevor-Roper, *Historical Essays*, Chapter xxix, 'Social Causes of the Great Rebellion'.

formidable weight of evidence to show that the origins of the struggle went back to a cleavage *within* the governing classes, that was determined by opposition to the methods of Stuart rule rather than by economic interest or belief in—as yet non-existent—'democratic principles'. Commenting on the fact that in many important respects 'there was no perceptible difference between the peers, knights, and gentlemen in Court offices and their counterparts in the Country opposition', he remarks,

> The conflict between the Court and the Country was therefore not rooted in social or economic contradictions. Fundamentally, it expressed a *political* opposition among the governing and wealthy members of the society, divided by their attachment or hostility to the operation of the authority and prerogative power of the crown. . . . Because the Court and the Country were formations within the governing class, no rigid barrier separated the two.[17]

It was only after the successful assertion of parliamentary rights in 1640-2 and the outbreak of war that this essentially conservative revolution was impelled by the very forces it had released in a much more radical direction.* Even in the middle years of the century, however, one finds, not a sharp division into opposing 'sides', but a series of fluctuating alliances of groups of persons that only at crucial moments—such as the outbreak of war or the trial and execution of the King—have even the appearance of massive cohesion. Not only were there sharp divisions within each camp, even after the war had started men changed sides, and there were those too—often the best—who were closer to some men of the opposing party than they were to many within their own. Looking back, we can see certain economic, political and intellectual movements that were to shape the future government of

* See Zagorin, *op. cit.*, Chapter 10 'Conclusion'.

the country and—broadly speaking—its political philosophy; but the closer one gets to the events of the time,
the broad stream of history is less apparent than the
swirls and eddies and the occasional whirlpool. For our
present purposes all we need to realize is that the civil
war was the sharp expression of a crisis—or, perhaps, of
overlapping crises*—within English society as a whole, or
at least in the more active and articulate part of it. In the
harsh confusion of immediate practical problems, with no
obvious and generally acceptable solutions in sight—for,

> when two authorities are up,
> Neither supreme, how soon confusion
> May enter 'twixt the gap of both and take
> The one by the other—

ideas were expressed that were to be influential or exemplary long after the particular struggle had ceased. Some
indeed of the writings of men directly involved in events
still demand that we should actively engage with them,
in our present. Putting this in another, and more limited,
way—Milton's political tracts, Clarendon's *History of the
Rebellion*, and Marvell's political poems, are not only
documents for historians.

(iii)

Of the writers of the period actively engaged in politics,
Milton was, I suppose, the greatest. Since I find Milton's
political polemic unsympathetic I must, to start with,
remind you that we are in fact dealing with a very great
man; a great man moreover whose work contains very

* For a criticism of the concept 'revolution' as applied to the seventeenth
century in England, see Peter Laslett, *The World we have Lost*, Chapter vii,
'Social Change and Revolution in the Traditional World'.

different strains and attitudes, so that there is bound to be something of contradiction and paradox in whatever we may say about him. Dr Johnson found no difficulty in disposing of Milton's politics:

> [His] republicanism was, I am afraid, founded in an envious hatred of greatness, and a sullen desire of independence; in petulance impatient of control, and pride disdainful of superiority. He hated monarchs in the State, and prelates in the Church; for he hated all whom he was required to obey. It is to be suspected that his predominant desire was to destroy rather than to establish, and that he felt not so much the love of liberty as repugnance to authority.

There is more to Milton's love of liberty than that, as anyone can see by reading *Areopagitica*, Milton's reply, in 1644, to Parliament's ordinance for licensing the Press in the previous year. That pamphlet is an obvious classic of its kind—which is to say that it is as relevant now as when it was first written.

> Well knows he who uses to consider, that our faith and knowledge thrives by exercise, as well as our limbs and complexion. Truth is compared in scripture to a streaming fountain; if her waters flow not in a perpetual progression, they sicken into a muddy pool of conformity and tradition. A man may be a heretic in the truth; and if he believes things only because his pastor says so, or the Assembly so determines, without knowing other reason, though his belief be true, yet the very truth he holds becomes his heresy.

From the author of *Areopagitica* we might expect a humane political attitude, and there are indeed qualities in Milton's republicanism that demand respect. In the *Second Defence of the English People* (1654), for example, after praising Cromwell, he pleads that he should not rule alone but associate with himself (I quote in Helen North's translation) 'men who are eminently modest, upright and brave, men who from the sight of so much death and slaughter before their very eyes have learned, not cruelty or hardness of heart, but justice, the fear of God, and compassion for the lot of mankind'.* It is not enough, he insists, to overthrow a corrupt government; men must learn the difficult arts of peace.

> If, having done with war, you neglect the arts of peace, if warfare is your peace and liberty, war your only virtue, your supreme glory, you will find, believe me, that peace itself is your greatest enemy. Peace itself will be by far your hardest war, and what you thought liberty will prove to be your servitude.

The task of government, he goes on, is not simply 'to devise the cleverest means of putting vast sums of money into the treasury', but 'to administer incorrupt justice to the people, to help those cruelly harassed and oppressed, and to render to every man promptly his own deserts'.† Finally, in recalling the value of some of Milton's public writings, we should remember that he wrote *The Ready and Easy Way to Establish a Free Commonwealth and the Excellence Thereof Compared with the Inconveniences and Dangers of Readmitting Kingship in this Nation* after General Monck had entered London in March, 1660, and that he published a second edition just before Charles II's Restoration in May. There is courage as well as idealism in Milton the pamphleteer, and Dr Johnson's dismissal—'his political notions were those of an acrimonious and surly republican'—just won't do.

All the same, there is a strain in Milton's political writing that makes against the humanistic virtues that he wished to promote. We may or may not agree with what he says about kings and the nature of government; but, as we have seen, when we try to assess the contribution

* Milton, *Complete Prose Works* (Yale University Press), Vol. IV, p. 674.
† *Op. cit.*, pp. 680-1.

of any piece of writing to the quality of political life, we have to take account not only of the *what* but the *how*: for the way in which a thing is spoken—the style, tone and general manner—is part of the total meaning, and makes its contribution, positive or negative, to political debate. It is with this in mind that I wish to speak, again briefly, of *The Tenure of Kings and Magistrates*, probably written during the King's trial in January, 1649, and published very shortly after his execution. It is of course a defence of the regicides. All power derives from 'the people' (left undefined: we shall come back to this later); when kings prove tyrants they may rightfully be deposed; Charles I had proved himself a tyrant; therefore . . .

I am not concerned here with the historical and theoretical bases of the argument, but with the style. It is of course highly rhetorical, with a good deal of name-calling, emotionally charged generalities, sweeping assertions, and forensic repetitions that add nothing to the sense, so that the argument is driven home rather by the strength of the blow than the sharpness of the point.

> Nor let them be discourag'd or deterr'd by any new Apostate Scarcrowes [the reference seems to be to crop-eared Prynne], who under show of giving counsel, send out their barking monitories and *mementoes*, empty of all else but the spleene of a frustrated Faction. For how can that pretended counsel bee either sound or faithfull, when they that give it, see not for madness and vexation of their ends lost, that those Statutes and Scriptures which both falsely and scandalously, they wrest against their Friends and Associates, would by sentence of the common adversarie, fall first and heaviest upon thir own heads. Neither let milde and tender dispositions be foolishly soften'd from thir duty and perseverance, with the unmasculine Rhetorick of any puling Priest or Chaplain. . . . Nor let any man be deluded by either the ignorance or the notorious hypocrisie and self-repugnance of our dancing Divines . . .*

* *Complete Prose* (Yale), Vol. III, pp. 194-5.

It is, as I have indicated, the style of the law-court rhetorician; and Milton had of course studied all the devices of classical rhetoric.[18] But it won't do to appeal, as one of the editors of the Yale Prose Works does,* to classical precedent for a justification of Milton's style. The question is whether he does anything with the devices he had learnt to make them more than rhetorical in the pejorative sense. Well yes, of course he does: he speaks with the voice of conviction, not as a hired advocate. But that does not prevent him from showing the vices of rhetoric. And one such vice is to make emotionally charged generalisations obscure the matter in hand so that conviction can be carried on a tide of feeling.

> Wee may from hence with more ease, and force of argument determin what a Tyrant is, and what the people may doe against him. A Tyrant whether by wrong or by right comming to the Crown, is he who regarding neither Law nor the common good, reigns onely for himself and his faction. . . . And because his power is great, his will boundless and exorbitant, the fulfilling whereof is for the most part accompanied with innumerable wrongs and oppressions of the people, murders, massachers, rapes, adulteries, desolation, and subversion of Citties and whole Provinces, look how great a good and happiness a just king is, so great a mischeife is a Tyrant. . . . †

The trouble with a sweeping indictment of this kind is that it admits no degrees of misrule: Milton speaks only of 'a tyrant', who is charged with a stock list of crimes, some of which—rapes, massacres—have no relevance to Charles I's personal rule in the 1630s. True, 'desolation, and subversion of cities' was one consequence of the civil war, but in strict logic that can't be attributed to the

---

* See Donald A. Roberts, Preface to *A Second Defence of the English People* (tr. Helen North), *Complete Prose* (Yale), Vol. IV, pp. 538-40.
† *Complete Works* (Yale), Vol. III, p. 212.

King alone, as though he had started the whole bitter business out of a deliberate plan of self-aggrandizement. As the anonymous author of *The Censure of the Rota* was to say to Milton in 1660, 'You trade altogether in universals, the region of deceits and fallacy, but never come so near particulars, as to let us know which among diverse things of the same kind you would be at'.*

Whatever the merits or demerits of Milton's case in *The Tenure*, abstractly conceived, the style itself is almost bound to lead to a false and damaging way of conceiving the political situation. Professor Merritt Hughes, in his admirable Introduction to Volume III of the Yale *Complete Prose*, comments on the drive and force of Milton's argument in *The Tenure*: '. . . at all levels he knew that his readers would have been disappointed if the fist of his logic had not been firm'.† 'The fist of his logic'—the phrase, though a conventional renaissance figure,‡ is unintentionally significant. The logic is undeviating—'a chain of deductions from the principle that all authority springs from the people'§; it is supported by all the resources of a polemical rhetoric; and all it ignores is the complex actuality of the historical moment. Just as Charles I, with all his grave shortcomings as well as his virtues, is presented as that spectral generic scarecrow, 'the tyrant', so some millions of Englishmen, with all their differing viewpoints, are subsumed under the head of 'the people', who may choose or reject, retain or depose. But who are 'the people'? In *The Second Defence of the English*

---

* *The Censure of the Rota upon Mr Milton's Book Entitled The Ready and Easie Way to Establish a Free Commonwealth.* Printed by Paul Giddy, Printer to the Rota, at the sign of the Windmill in Turnagain Lane, 1660.

† Milton, *Complete Prose* (Yale), Vol. III, ed. Merritt Y. Hughes, Chapter vii, 'The Style of Milton's Regicide Tracts', p. 131.

‡ Wilbur Samuel Howell, *Logic and Rhetoric in England, 1500-1700*: see index, 'logic as the closed fist'.

§ Merritt Hughes, *loc. cit.*

People (1654) Milton was to answer the charge that the Independents who seized power did not represent the majority of Englishmen by asserting that virtue and wisdom were more important than mere numbers.

> Those whose power lies in wisdom, experience, industry, and virtue will, in my opinion, however small their number, be a majority and prove more powerful in ballotting everywhere than any mere number, however great.*

There are circumstances in which one can assent to the tenor of this; that is, in those fields where virtue, or wisdom, or even mere know-how are the essential criteria: that is to say, in all those forms of human association for a specific purpose, whether a monastery or a scientific laboratory, where one doesn't count the heads of the unqualified in order to determine where authority shall lie. But it is dangerous doctrine in politics. As Don M. Wolfe says:

> Despite his high motive, therefore, Milton not only justified an illegal action but renounced the democratic principle; namely the right of the people to determine the actions of its government, the same right for which he had repeatedly argued. . . . [He] would not grant the right of a people to be governed by a tyrant. When the English people clamoured for a king, at that moment, Milton felt, coercion by the enlightened few was entirely justified. It was coercion on the side of progress. It was coercion on behalf of the *ultimate* state of public opinion.†

It is a cruel—and recurring—dilemma, as we have seen in times nearer to our own. Trotsky, when deprived of power, bitterly denounced 'substitutism'—that is, the

---

* Helen North's translation. *Complete Prose* (Yale), Vol. IV, p. 636.

† Don M. Wolfe, *Milton in the Puritan Revolution*, p. 230. That the problem Milton failed to solve was shared by many of the most high-minded of his contemporaries is shown by Christopher Hill in a chapter of his book on Cromwell aptly headed 'The People of England and the People of God'—*God's Englishman: Oliver Cromwell and the English Revolution*, Chapter viii.

substitution of a party for the working classes, of the party organization for the party, of a central committee for the organization, and of a dictator for the committee.* But Trotsky himself, in his *History of the Russian Revolution*, claimed that in 1917 the Bolsheviks, although a minority, 'really represented' the people, the proletariat of the future.

> It would seem (he said) as though the soviets, elected by a part of the city's population, should have less power and influence than the dumas, elected by the whole population. But the dialectic of the revolutionary process has demonstrated that in certain historic conditions the part is incomparably greater than the whole.†

One cannot avoid the conclusion that the secular creed that Trotsky shared with Lenin was entangled in the same contradictions as the religiously toned aspirations of the English revolutionaries of the seventeenth century.‡

The comparison is not entirely fair to Milton, because he knew—and had stated in *The Tenure*—that 'none can love freedom heartily but good men'; and in his later political writings sweeping assertion gives way to a tempered sense of the difficulty of finding men who are worthy representatives of 'the people'—something that in turn leads on to the tragic patience of *Samson Agonistes*.[19] But that is another story. It does not, I think, affect what I have said about the method of political argument in *The Tenure of Kings and Magistrates*.

* See the first two volumes of Isaac Deutscher's biography of Trotsky, *The Prophet Armed*, and *The Prophet Unarmed*, both *passim*.

† Leon Trotsky, *History of the Russian Revolution*, translated by Max Eastman, Vol. II, p. 303.

‡ See Isaac Deutscher's *The Unfinished Revolution: Russia 1917-1967*, and E. H. Carr's *1917: Before and After*. An early perception of the dictatorial tendencies inherent in Leninism was shown by Rosa Luxemburg; see *The Russian Revolution* and *Leninism or Marxism* (Ann Arbor paperback).

I hope I have made clear the point of view from which I have asked you to consider Milton the public man. I am not saying that in those crucial years he should not have taken a republican stand: I am saying that in his political writings there is not the tension, the recognition of conflicting claims, that you find in Marvell—who was as capable of decisive choice and effective action as Milton himself.

CHAPTER IV

Tension and Commitment: The Falkland Circle, Clarendon, and Marvell

(i)

IN beginning this lecture it is impossible not to recall T. S. Eliot's phrase for the men of the seventeenth century whom he commemorates in *Little Gidding*—'united in the strife that divided them'. In the poem they are united in a mind that can extract from past history a fuller liberty for living in the present, and—as the poem reminds us—when our past was their present no such reconcilement was possible. Falkland and Clarendon, although they began as parliamentarians, ended as King's men; Marvell, although he had been a friend of royalists and was to continue as a member of parliament after the Restoration, was, during his most creative period, either withdrawn from active politics or a committed Cromwellian. But even whilst they were alive and engaged in confused and bitterly divisive politics, they brought to public affairs qualities of intellect and imagination that set them apart from men with one-track minds. What united them was the kind of integrity that gives to political commitments a deeper resonance.

More than twenty years ago I published an essay on Clarendon in which I tried to explain my admiration for his great *History*,* to define Clarendon's way of presenting events and the actors in those events, and to indicate the principles that guide and inform his vision; and I will not

* In *Scrutiny*, XV, 2, Spring 1948; republished in *Further Explorations*.

now repeat myself more than is necessary to bring out the relevance of the man and his work to the matters we are considering in these lectures. First of all, to remind ourselves of his early milieu is to bring out the connexion between a particular style in politics and what lies behind style—in this case a network of personal friendships and a tradition. In the *Life* that supplements the *History* he says of himself:

> He was often heard to say, that, 'next the immediate blessing and providence of God Almighty, which had preserved him throughout the whole course of his life . . . he owed all the little he knew, and the little good that was in him, to the friendships and conversation he had still been used to, of the most excellent men in their several kinds that lived in that age; by whose learning, and information, and instruction, he formed his studies, and mended his understanding; and by whose gentleness and sweetness of behaviour, and justice, and virtue, and example, he formed his manners, subdued that pride, and suppressed that heat and passion, he was naturally transported with.' . . . And [he] used often to say, 'that he never was so proud, or thought himself so good a man, as when he was the worst man in the company'.*

The acquaintances of Clarendon's early London years included Selden (whom he continued to admire even when they had parted company in politics), and Ben Jonson, whose views on the moral and intellectual weight needed by statesmen are clear enough from his completely unservile verse epistles to his noble patrons. Even more important were those whom Clarendon goes on to mention in terms that, written by the seasoned statesman, have still something of the freshness that accompanies the first meeting of kindred minds—Lucius Cary Lord

---

* *The Life of Edward Earl of Clarendon . . . Written by Himself* (Oxford, 1759). Most of the quotations from *The History of the Rebellion* and the *Life* used in this section can be found in *Selections from Clarendon*, ed. G. Huehns (World Classics).

Falkland, Sheldon, Earles, Hales, Chillingworth and others who came to Falkland's house at Great Tew,

> So that his house was a university in a less volume; whither they came not so much for repose as study; and to examine and refine those grosser propositions, which laziness and consent made current in vulgar conversation.

It is well known that this group has a special place in the history of religious toleration in England, and we should remember it here not only because religion and politics were so closely connected in the seventeenth century. Falkland himself 'was so great an enemy to that passion and uncharitableness, which he saw produced, by difference of opinion, in matters of religion, that in all those disputations with priests, and others of the Roman church, he affected to manifest all possible civility to their persons, and estimation of their parts'. 'In all those controversies, he had so dispassioned a consideration, such a candour in his nature, and so profound a charity in his conscience, that in those points in which he was in his own judgment most clear, he never thought the worse, or in any degree declined the familiarity of those who were of another mind, which without question is an excellent temper for the propagation and advancement of Christianity.' Chillingworth ('whose only unhappiness proceeded from his sleeping too little, and thinking too much'), who described the Civil War as 'Publicans and Sinners on the one side, against Scribes and Pharisees on the other',* wrote *The Religion of Protestants* at Great Tew.[20] John Hales, Regius Professor of Greek at Oxford, Fellow of Merton and Eton, declared 'that nobody would conclude another man to be damned, who did not wish

---

* J. A. R. Marriott, *The Life and Times of Lucius Cary, Viscount Falkland*, p. 248.

him so'. It is worth pausing on Hales for a moment. His small *Tract concerning Schisme and Schismatiques* (1642), pleading for a greater toleration and communion between Christians who are agreed on the fundamentals of their faith, begins: 'Heresy and Schism, as they are commonly used, are two theological scare-crows, with which they who use to uphold a party in religion, use to fright away such, as making enquiry into it, are ready to relinquish it, if it appear either erroneous or suspicious'. Now Hales was a great admirer of Shakespeare, remarking 'that there was no subject of which any Poet ever writ, but he would produce it much better treated of in Shakespeare'.* He himself was admired by Clarendon ('he was one of the least men in the kingdom; and one of the greatest scholars in Europe'). And many years later, Marvell, in his witty and deeply committed plea for toleration, *The Rehearsal Transprosed*, before quoting from Hales' *Tract*, was to say of its author, 'I account it no small honour to have grown up into some part of his acquaintance, and convers'd a while with the living remains of one of the clearest heads and best-prepared breasts in Christendom'.†
It is by such unspectacular connexions—mind working on mind—which usually do not get much attention in the history books, that men achieve such progress as is possible.

In politics the Falkland-Hyde group were constitutionalists: Parliament was part of the constitution, but so was the Crown: each had its rights and duties. Falkland and Hyde were both active supporters of the work of the first session of the Long Parliament, which cut back the

---

* The remark first appears in Dryden's essay *Of Dramatic Poesy*. See David Nichol Smith, *Characters from the Histories and Memoirs of the Seventeenth Century*, p. 297.
† Marvell, *Works*, ed. A. B. Grosart, Vol. II, p. 125.

encroachments of the royal prerogative. It was only when they saw a new kind of unconstitutional absolutism developing within Parliament itself that they drew towards the King. Hyde's position has been fully described by Mr B. H. G. Wormald. Writing of the period immediately preceding the King's withdrawal to York, he says:

> Hyde and Pym had, in truth, all along been saying the same thing. They had been saying that it was the King and the King alone who was responsible for the line of policy pursued by Parliament. Both men were bent on persuading him of the fact, the difference between the two being that Pym was using the method of threats, while Hyde used the method of reason. . . . There was, therefore, still all the difference in the world between Hyde and the Royalists proper. . . . If he is a Royalist in the eyes of Parliament as then led, he was not a Royalist in his own eyes or in those of the Royalists such as there were at this time. Employing the terms sanctioned by historical usage, it is correct to describe him as remaining as much a Parliamentarian as ever.[21]

As for Falkland, he 'contracted such a reverence for parliaments', says Clarendon, 'that he thought it really impossible they could ever produce mischief or inconvenience to the kingdom; or that the kingdom could be tolerably happy in the intermission of them'. They were, in short, constitutionally speaking, men of the middle way —though what it means to be a man of the middle way in politics is a question that we shall have an opportunity of thinking about later: it does *not* mean lukewarmness or an inability to make up one's mind. Meanwhile we may note that if both men respected custom and the Common Law, they were not mere legalists. Nothing is more marked in Clarendon's account of the ways in which matters of state were, or ought to be, conducted, than the assumption that the statesman needs to combine shrewd practical ability with moral principle, 'and integrity above all'. It is this ability to see general principles at work in confused particular circumstances that makes *The History of the Rebellion* a so much greater work than, say, Burnet's *History of his Own Times*. Burnet, I am sure, was a good man, who did what he saw ought to be done; but he gives the sense at times of being too busily engaged in the politics of the present: he has not Clarendon's much larger perspective.

We are not here concerned, then, with the history of the times or with the individual histories of the men of whom I have been speaking. What we are concerned with is Clarendon's *History*, with a way of writing that not only tells us a good deal about the political attitudes of a particular man and the milieu of his formative years, but from which we can learn something about historical and political writing in general. The *History* has its weaknesses and limitations, but these are far outweighed by its positive qualities.

It is a commonplace that one of Clarendon's great merits as a writer is seen in his character sketches.* They all deserve to be widely known, but since selection is necessary a passage from the account of Falkland will serve as an example.

From the entrance into this unnatural war, his natural cheerfulness and vivacity grew clouded, and a kind of sadness and dejection of spirit stole upon him, which he had never been used to; yet being one of those who believed that one battle would end all differences, and that there would be so great a victory on one side, that the other would be compelled to submit to any conditions from the victor, (which supposition and conclusion generally sunk into the minds of most men,

* For some acute criticism see David Nichol Smith, *Characters from the Histories and Memoirs of the Seventeenth Century*, pp. xxxix ff.

and prevented the looking after many advantages, that might then have been laid hold of,) he resisted those indispositions, *et in luctu, bellum inter remedia erat.* But after the king's return from Brentford, and the furious resolution of the two houses not to admit any treaty for peace, those indispositions, which had before touched him, grew into a perfect habit of uncheerfulness; and he, who had been so exactly unreserved and affable to all men, that his face and countenance was always present, and vacant to his company, and held any cloudiness, and less pleasantness of the visage, a kind of rudeness or incivility, became, on a sudden, less communicable; and then, very sad, pale, and exceedingly affected with the spleen. In his clothes and habit, which he had intended before always with more neatness, and industry, and expense, than is usual to so great a mind, he was not now only incurious, but too negligent; and in his reception of suitors, and the necessary or casual addresses to his place, so quick, and sharp, and severe, that there wanted not some men, (who were strangers to his nature and disposition,) who believed him proud and imperious, from which no mortal man was ever more free.

The truth is, that as he was of a most incomparable gentleness, application, and even demissiveness and submission to good, and worthy, and entire men, so he was naturally (which could not but be more evident in his place, which objected him to another conversation and intermixture, than his own election had done) *adversus malos injucundus*; and was so ill a dissembler of his dislike and disinclination to ill men, that it was not possible for such not to discern it. There was once, in the house of commons, such a declared acceptation of the good service an eminent member had done to them, and, as they said, to the whole kingdom, that it was moved, he being present, 'that the speaker might, in the name of the whole house, give him thanks; and then, that every member might, as a testimony of his particular acknowledgment, stir or move his hat towards him'; the which (though not ordered) when very many did, the lord Falkland, (who believed the service itself not to be of that moment, and that an honourable and generous person could not have stooped to it for any recompense,) instead of moving his hat, stretched both his arms out, and clasped his hands together upon the crown of his hat, and held it close down to his head; that all men might see, how odious that flattery was to him, and the very approbation of the person, though at that time most popular.

The vocabulary is slightly, but not obtrusively, latinate, the tone that of grave, weighty consideration. The sentences are ample and leisurely, and many words are nearly, but not quite, synonyms. But the long periods are controlled, as in the last sentence (some 150 words), which contains the whole incident in the Commons; and once you get the sense of it it is easy to read aloud. Even the five parentheses contrive without awkwardness to bring more into the attention and hold it there while the main sense goes on. Thus the first sentence starts with the conduct of a particular person, but in the parenthesis Clarendon moves from the particular to a reflection on the situation at large. And this kind of movement—from persons to events and the statesman's reflections on events —is characteristic of the *History* as a whole. You are conscious of events brought to a focus and pondered in a particular mind; there is a point of view; but the actuality seen from this view-point, although necessarily limited, is still very complex and very human. The total effect is to make the reader conscious of an interaction between persons—with their particular quirks, interests, motives and principles—and the larger tragic pattern. 'He understood . . . that the study of politics is in fact always also the study of politicians.'* I have said elsewhere that Clarendon has some of the qualities of a great novelist. Obviously he is entirely without, say, Henry James's

* H. R. Trevor-Roper, 'Clarendon and the Great Rebellion', *Historical Essays*, p. 247. See also the same writer's 'Clarendon and the Practice of History', in *Milton and Clarendon*, by F. R. Fogle and H. R. Trevor-Roper (Williams Andrews Clark Memorial Library, University of California, Los Angeles, 1965).

sharp defining imagery, and he is in general incapable of the *dramatic* rendering of moral qualities that you find in George Eliot or Jane Austen. But he does have something of the novelist's art—the ability not only to define a particular kind of character, but to extend and refine the ways in which we see our world.

What is in question however is not only an ability to give vivid and discriminating character sketches. Clarendon's *manner* throughout is a way of conveying a particular attitude to politics and to life. We see this when he discusses some of the difficulties of a statesman.

And it cannot easily be expressed, nor comprehended by any who have not felt the weight and burden of the envy, which naturally attends upon those promotions, which seem to be *per saltum*, how great straits and difficulties such ministers are forced to wrestle with, and by which the charges, with which they are intrusted, must proportionably suffer, let the integrity and wisdom of the men be what it can be supposed to be. Neither is the patience, temper and dexterity, to carry a man through those straits, easily attained; it being very hard, in the morning of preferment, to keep an even temper of mind, between the care to preserve the dignity of the place committed to him, (without which he shall expose himself to a thousand unchaste attempts, and dishonour the judgment that promoted him, by appearing too vile for such a trust,) and the caution, that his nature be not really exalted to an overweening pride and folly, upon the privilege of his place; which will expose him to much more contempt than the former; and therefore [is], with a more exact guard upon a man's self, to be avoided: the errors of gentleness and civility being much more easily reformed, as well as endured, than the other of arrogance and ostentation.

The best provision that such men can make for their voyage, besides a stock of innocency that cannot be impaired, and a firm confidence in God Almighty, that he will never suffer that innocency be utterly oppressed, or notoriously defamed, is, an expectation of those gusts and storms of rumour,

detraction, and envy; and a resolution not to be over sensible
of all calumnies, unkindness, or injustice; but to believe, that,
by being preferred before other men, they have an obligation
upon them, to suffer more than other men would do; and that
the best way to convince scandals, and misreports, is, by neglect-
ing them, to appear not to have deserved them. And there is not
a more troublesome passion, or that often draws more inconveniences with it, than that which proceeds from the indignation of being unjustly calumniated, and from the pride of an
upright conscience; when men cannot endure to be spoken
ill of, if they have not deserved it: in which distemper, though
they free themselves from the errors, or infirmities, with
which they were traduced, they commonly discover others,
of which they had never been suspected. In a word, let no man
think, that is once entered into the list, he can by any skill,
or comportment, prevent these conflicts and assaults; or by
any stubborn or impetuous humour, suppress and prevail over
them: but let him look upon it as purgatory he is unavoidably
to pass through, and depend upon Providence, and time, for
a vindication; and by performing all the duties of his place to
the end with justice, integrity, and uprightness, give all men
cause to believe, he was worthy of it the first hour, which is a
triumph very lawful to be affected.

Clarendon is here discussing the obvious difficulties of
those whose rise to great place has been sudden. He first
disposes of the twin dangers to which such men are exposed—the danger of an over-familiarity that would expose the office itself to contempt or abuse, and the danger
of pride; and he discriminates between them—of the two
the latter is the worse. How is one to comport oneself
in such an exposed position? The second paragraph begins
with an unfeigned emphasis on innocence and trust in
God, combined with a disillusioned, but not cynical,
recognition of what you have to expect in great place—
uncynical because not paraded: this is simply the way the
world goes. From this, which a number of honest states-

men might have written, Clarendon goes on to one of those
aperçus that we learn to expect in the *History*: 'And there
is not a more troublesome passion, or that often draws
more inconveniences with it, than that which proceeds
from the indignation of being unjustly calumniated. . . .'
Discussion of public matters as Clarendon conducts it
opens towards a world of psychological insight and moral
principle. Reverberations such as these give an extra
dimension to the *History*.

The History of the Rebellion is, then, very much an individual achievement; but it is much more than just that.
In the essay to which I have referred I said that 'what is
shown by Clarendon's firm grasp of the personal factor in
history and his shrewd and subtle appraisal of character, is
that he was the product of a society within which there was
a highly developed sense of the person, a society for which
personal and moral issues mattered, and which possessed
a language in which these issues could be intelligently
discussed.' His work is related to a rich culture in the
ordinary sense of the word. He took for granted 'how
necessary a good education and knowledge of men is to
make a wise man, at least a man fit for business'; and,
pondering the fact that the King could not find all the
able councillors he needed from the aristocracy, he remarks—and we should notice the qualities he puts stress
on—'It were to be wished, that persons of the greatest
birth, honour, and fortune, would take that care of themselves by education, industry, literature, and a love of
virtue, to surpass all other men in knowledge, and all
other qualifications necessary for great actions'. But even
in the passages we have looked at it is plain that more
than formal education is involved. The 'culture' in question is one in which literature and learning, and a knowledge of men and affairs, are sifted in discussion that is

at once free and ranging and *concerned*. It is, basically, the culture of Great Tew, for as Nichol Smith says, 'The school in which [Clarendon] learned most was the circle of his friends'.* We may recall here Matthew Arnold's praise of Falkland's 'lucidity of mind and largeness of temper'. He had, says Arnold, 'the historic sense in politics; an aversion to root-and-branch work, to what he called "great mutations". . . . He and his friends, by their heroic and hopeless stand against the inadequate ideals dominant in their time, kept open their communications with the future.'† Not all the wisdom of the age was to be found at Tew, but much that was best in the thought of the time was represented there: a sense of history and an appeal to reason, a spirit of free and charitable enquiry, a tone and temper in debate that was far removed from that of the unquestioning partisans, the fanatics and the simplifiers. It is to these men and to the qualities they embodied that *The History of the Rebellion* is in some sense a monument.

(ii)

The greatness of Marvell's 'An Horatian Ode upon Cromwell's Return from Ireland' is as universally admitted as the interpretations of it are diverse. It would be sufficient for my present purposes if, for a few people, I could throw a little light on the greatness of that one poem, which has a continuing life of its own independent of all historical considerations. But in order to bring out its relevance as a mode of public speech it is necessary to put it in its setting, and to look both before and after before turning to the poem itself.

* *Op. cit.*, p. xxxix.
† Matthew Arnold, 'Falkland', in *Mixed Essays*.

Marvell did not fight in the Civil War (he was abroad for much of the time); although 'puritan' by upbringing, he had royalist sympathies; and although he took service with Fairfax in the 1650s, became tutor to a ward of Cromwell's, Assistant Latin Secretary with Milton, and finally M.P. for Hull in 1659, he continued in Parliament after the Restoration, even though in opposition to the Court party and as an advocate of toleration. His final verdict on the Civil War, in *The Rehearsal Transprosed*, was that in it 'Hell broke loose'. 'Upon considering all, I think the cause was too good to have been fought for. Men ought to have trusted God; they ought and might have trusted the King with that whole matter. . . . For men may spare their pains where nature is at work, and the world will not go the faster for our driving.' Clearly he is not an easy man to attach a label to; and his political convictions are not easy to define.

Professor John Wallace, in *Destiny his Choice: the Loyalism of Andrew Marvell*, has argued persuasively that Marvell was a moderate constitutionalist, though, as he makes clear, in those troubled years 'moderation was an extremely active virtue, unrelated to neutrality'. The 'loyalists' were men whose loyalties were to the constitution—the 'idea' of the constitution—rather than to any abstract ideal of royalism or republicanism or democracy. When the second civil war ended there were very many men who, whatever their previous commitments, thought and felt in similar ways. All forms of government had been destroyed; the only possible attitude was a waiting on events; meanwhile government had to be carried on. 'Loyalism', says Wallace, 'was created from chaos, in those moments of desperation when the only conceivable action is the performance of daily routine'. After the execution of the King traditional parliamentarians who remained in England might accept the new power, but they looked for it to be regularized in a constitution. They looked to Cromwell, first as the only guarantor of public order—for some sort of power was necessary if men were not to start killing each other again—and then, as successive experiments in government broke down, as the likely founder of a new dynasty. It was because the 'loyalists' thought in these terms that after Cromwell's death they could without inconsistency accept the Restoration settlement as part of a providential plan. Putting it another way, that was how the logic of events had worked out. If Marvell was a 'loyalist' in this sense—and I think Professor Wallace's case is sound, even though it is possible to disagree on some details—he was not very far from the position ascribed by Mr Wormald to Clarendon.*

'An Horatian Ode' belongs to the early summer of 1650. As we shall see, it is not a poem that lends itself to straightforward description in terms of a particular political standpoint; but it is convenient here to look forward to two later poems that are straightforward praise of the Lord Protector—'The First Anniversary of the Government under O. C.' (written December, 1664), and 'A Poem upon the Death of O. C.' (1658)—for they too tell us something about Marvell's attitude towards public affairs, even though by contrast they bring out the incomparable greatness of the Ode. Read out of context and without reference to Marvell's conviction of the need for strong but constitutional government, 'The First Anniversary' might strike the modern reader as a little fulsome; and of necessity the praise of Cromwell hasn't the counterbalancing weight of the feeling for Charles that we find in the earlier poem. But it isn't a *simple* panegyric

* B. H. G. Wormald, *Clarendon: Politics, Historiography and Religion*, 1640-1660. See especially pp. 150 and 220.

—like Waller's or Dryden's*; the praise is related to serious and more-than-political standards. Anticipating Coleridge's remark that 'not without celestial observations can even terrestrial charts be accurately constructed', Marvell insists that earthly laws should be related to an ideal model:

> While indefatigible *Cromwell* hyes
> And cuts his way still nearer to the Skyes,
> Learning a Musique in the Region clear,
> To tune this lower to that higher Sphere.

In other words, the best ruler is the private man ('Resigning up thy Privacy so dear, / To Turn the headstrong People's Charioteer'), who has tried to put himself in order ('first growing to thy self a Law'), before assuming political power. And although Marvell clearly sees Cromwell as the destined leader, perhaps as King, he still sees government as a balance of forces in which liberty and authority each have their place—'Founding a firm State by Proportions true'.

> 'Tis not a Freedom, that where All command;
> Nor Tyranny, where One does them withstand:
> But who of both the Bounders knows to lay
> Him as their Father must the State obey. . . .
>
> That sober Liberty which men may have. . . .

It is oddly like Dryden at times—for example in the distrust of sects and fanatics (ll. 293-320); but of course Dryden comes down more firmly on the conservative side. Marvell may have come to believe that Cromwell should

---

* Waller, 'A Panegyric to my Lord Protector, of the Present Greatness, and Joint Interest of his Highness, and this Nation' (1655); Dryden, 'Heroic Stanzas, Consecrated to the Memory of his Highness, Oliver, Late Lord Protector of this Commonwealth, &c' (1658).

accept the crown, but if we think of what monarchy meant in most of Europe in the seventeenth century, he is decidedly anti-monarchist: he believes in a mixed government in which constitutional opposition has its proper place. The commonwealth is compared to a building composed of different parts with different functions.

> The Common-wealth does through their Centers all
> Draw the Circumf'rence of the publique Wall;
> The crossest* Spirits here do take their part,
> Fast'ning the Contignation which they thwart;
> And they, whose Nature leads them to divide,
> Uphold, this one, and that the other Side;
> But the most Equal† still sustein the Height,
> And they as Pillars keep the Work upright;
> While the resistance of opposed Minds,
> The Fabrick as with Arches stronger binds,
> Which on the Basis of a Senate free,
> Knit by the Roofs protecting weight agree.[22]

In 'A Poem upon the Death of O. C.', which clearly shows Marvell's affection for Cromwell, much the same political themes are repeated, though less effectively. There is the same admiration for the fact that the private man was not lost in the public figure:

> For he no duty by his height excus'd,
> Nor though a *Prince* to be a *Man* refus'd.

The poem emphasizes his domestic affection, especially towards the daughter who had died just before him, and you are made to feel that it was only his personal integrity that allowed him to accomplish his almost superhuman tasks.

> If so indulgent to his own, how deare
> To him the children of the Highest were?

* *Sc.* most contrary.
† *Sc.* best qualified *and* most equitable or just.

86

What prudence more than humane did he need
To keep so deare, so diff'ring minds agreed?

It is with Cromwell's example in mind that the poet looks forward to a time 'When truth shall be allow'd, and faction cease'.

But it is time to turn to 'An Horatian Ode'. It is a paradoxical poem, if only because, ostensibly in celebration of Cromwell, the stanzas that everyone remembers are a deeply moving tribute to Charles.

> *He* nothing common did or mean
> Upon that memorable Scene:
> But with his keener Eye
> The Axes edge did try:
>
> Nor call'd the *Gods* with vulgar spight
> To vindicate his helpless Right,
> But bow'd his comely Head,
> Down as upon a Bed.

The poem has of course been seen as straightforwardly Cromwellian, with an almost incidental tribute to a fallen adversary. It has also been said (by C. H. Sisson, in *Art and Action*, 'Reflections on Marvell's Ode') that 'the death of the King was the true subject of the poem': even the apparent praise of Cromwell is in fact irony directed at a man whose work 'appears to Marvell primarily as one of destruction, not of liberation'. As a third alternative we have the view of M. Pierre Legouis, that the poem 'has the merit of complete independence, nay, of an almost inhuman aloofness'.* None of this will do. Nor need we be troubled by the vein of paradox in the poem if we remember that one of Marvell's favourite poetic forms was the dialogue, used for the serious debate of

* C. H. Sisson, 'Reflections on Marvell's Ode', *Art and Action*, pp. 12-13; Pierre Legouis, *Andrew Marvell* (1965), p. 14.

moral issues, each of which is given due weight, as in 'A Dialogue between the Resolved Soul and Created Pleasure', and 'A Dialogue between the Soul and the Body'; that different poems, apparently written within a fairly short period, offer fundamentally different or opposed points of view, regarding such matters as the human significance of Nature's 'wild and fragrant innocence' and the value of Nature methodized in formal gardens and properly laid out estates, or the claims of retirement and solitude, and of society and action; and, finally, that the best of his poetry is distinguished by a serious wit, of which T. S. Eliot, in a famous essay, said, 'it implies a constant inspection and criticism of experience. It involves, probably, a recognition, implicit in the expression of every experience, of other kinds of experience which are possible.'

It may not be a universal law that poets make poetry out of quarrels with themselves, but all great poetry contains somewhere in itself 'opposite and discordant qualities', and Marvell's is very plainly a poetry of conflict as, say, Dryden's is not, even though Dryden more than once changed his mind. Christopher Hill, in his essay 'Society and Andrew Marvell' (in *Puritanism and Revolution*), suggests that 'Marvell's poetry is shot through with the consciousness of a conflict between subjective and objective, between the idea and the reality'. And although I think that he is wrong when he links this—even 'very indirectly'—with the social and political problems of the time, I am certainly ready to follow him when he says that 'in many of the poems Marvell is concerned to show the mutual indispensability of apparent opposites'. As a more recent writer, Joseph Summers, has said, Marvell's structural forms 'often dramatize the movements towards decision or judgement which underlie the poems. Rival claims are fully weighed, and the judgements are made with full knowledge.'*

'An Horatian Ode' is a great political poem because it is great poetry. It has energy and variety; by which I do not mean only that it records an enormous number of different attitudes and activities—some at the level of actuality, such as the young men taking down the armour from the wall, Cromwell in his garden, Charles on the scaffold,

> While round the armed Bands
> Did clap their bloody hands;

some seen through a reflective and witty intelligence, as the Pict, whose mind is of more than one colour, like his plaid; some introduced by way of metaphor and image. The verse form—an imitation of a measure of Horace—that looks so regular, is in fact an extremely supple vehicle for narrative, moral and political observations, vividly rendered scenes and actions, pathos and metaphysical wit. The *energy*, then, is largely a matter of the changing demands made on the reader by the constant shifts of tone, imagery and rhythm.

> 'Tis Madness to resist or blame
> The force of angry Heavens flame:
> And, if we would speak true,
> Much to the Man is due.

* Joseph H. Summers, 'Andrew Marvell: Private Taste and Public Judgement'; in *Stratford-upon-Avon Studies*, II, *Metaphysical Poetry* (ed. D. J. Palmer and Malcolm Bradbury). In 'The Actor and the Man of Action: Marvell's Horatian Ode', *The Critical Survey* (N.Z.), Winter 1967, Professor C. K. Stead sees the 'objective' elements of conflict presented in the poem as part of a 'subjective' conflict in Marvell's own mind that ranges beyond the overt political subject. See also Andor Gomme, 'The Teasingness of Andrew Marvell', *Oxford Review*, 8 and 9 (1968).

Who, from his private Gardens, where
He liv'd reserved and austere,
    As if his highest plot
    To plant the Bergamot,

Could by industrious Valour climbe
To ruine the great Work of Time,
    And cast the Kingdome old
    Into another Mold.

The modulations of tone and rhythm in those dozen lines convey a wealth of pondered comment.

With this we come back to the poem's apparent doubleness, the puzzle it may seem to present about the exact nature of Marvell's attitude. In the stanzas on Charles's execution that I have already quoted there is an active mind at work (Margoliouth noted the concealed pun: *acies* = eyesight *and* the axe's edge), but that reinforces rather than disturbs the deep human feeling. But again, the context inhibits any sense of mere pathos for 'the Royal Actor':

Though Justice against Fate complain,
And plead the Antient Rights in vain:
    But those do hold or break
    As Men are strong or weak.

Nature that hateth emptiness,
Allows of penetration less:
    And therefore must make room
    Where greater Spirits come.

This obvious balance of sympathy leads back to the point I made about the tone and rhythm. The controlled ease of movement, as the poem moves through such diversity, suggests an even distribution of attention. There is praise for Cromwell, but there is also criticism: 'So *restless*

Cromwell could not cease / In the *inglorious* Arts of Peace'
(my italics). And how are we to take the ending? Marvell
comes down on the side of Cromwell (I think Wallace is
right in this, though the view has been challenged), but
there is a sombre realism in his appraisal of the situation.

> But thou the Wars and Fortunes Son
> March indefatigably on;
> > And for the last effect
> > Still keep the Sword erect:
>
> Besides the force it has to fright
> The Spirits of the shady Night,
> > The same *Arts* that did *gain*
> > A *Pow'r* must it *maintain*.

In short, the poem is an attempt to grasp in its wholeness
a crisis or climacteric in history.

There is a further point. The subject is Cromwell; but
the undercurrent that gives strength and emotional force
to the poem is a sense of Fate, of what, things being as
they were, they were bound to be. Cromwell is as irre-
sistible as 'the three-fork'd Lightning'; he 'burns through
the air' like a fiery portent; he represents 'angry Heaven's
flame', which it is 'Madness to resist'; he is the Fate
against which Justice complains. It is this sense of inevitable destiny, of a great historical process at work, from
which much of the imaginative force and grandeur of the
poem springs—

> But thou the Wars and Fortunes Son
> March indefatigably on . . .

In this feeling for the historically inevitable, the poem is
plainly by the man who wrote that 'men may spare their
pains when nature is at work, and the world will not go

the faster for our driving'. But in 'An Horatian Ode' this semi-Calvinist attitude is qualified—and here we have one more reconciliation of opposites—by a real feeling for human personality as an instrument and necessary agent of the more-than-personal movement of history. Both the Cromwell and the Charles of the poem have the ability to withdraw into their personal selves, to a world of private calm, 'reserved and austere', or private agony and personal courage.

There is no need to claim for Marvell political infallibility. But the keen interest in, yet detachment from, public affairs, the swift play of mind, the precision, balance and sureness of touch, the deep but controlled feeling, the sense of the complexity of things and of the impossibility of making simple judgments of tangled and tragic situations—these qualities combine to make 'An Horatian Ode' the greatest political poem in the language. The tension between conflicting claims that we find in it is not the same as vacillation; and, so far as the political situation of the 1650s is concerned, it is very far from implying a paralysing 'neutrality'. Joseph Summers, in the essay from which I have quoted, speaks disparagingly of 'a critical assumption quite widespread a few years ago that the most "mature" (and therefore literarily desirable) human attitude is an ironic embracement of all contradictory impulses—a condition of complete paralysis costing not less than everything'. That is not what I mean at all. The quality I am referring to is something positive, even though difficult to define. It is perhaps indicated by the psychiatrist Rollo May, in his book *Love and Will*, when he remarks that 'the moral problem is not simply a matter of believing in one's convictions and acting on them, for people's convictions can be as dominating and destructive, if not more so, than mere pragmatic positions. The moral problem is the relentless endeavour to find one's own convictions and at the same time to admit that there will always be in them an element of self-aggrandizement and distortion. Here is where Socrates' principle of humility is essential. . . .'*

Humility, I suppose, is closely connected with openness to experience, the willingness not to impose a pre-determined pattern on life's diversity. And if we want to draw a general moral from the particular case before us, we can say that tension, a sense of complexity, is not incompatible with firm commitment, or, at the very least, a clear approach to commitment. And just as in the non-political poems Marvell shows a strong feeling for what is ordered, seemly, civilized, without disowning the energies of untamed Nature, so his Cromwellian poems —and notably the Ode—reach down into the pre-political—'the stratum', as T. S. Eliot has said, 'down to which any sound political thinking must push its roots, and from which it must derive its nourishment'.† Putting all this in another way: in 'An Horatian Ode' the civilized voice is the voice of a deep commitment to life. That is why to know it more or less by heart is to find nourishment for our own public and political attitudes—whether these are Left, Right, or Centre.

* Rollo May, *Love and Will*, p. 158.
† T. S. Eliot, *To Criticize the Critic*, 'The Literature of Politics', p. 144.

CHAPTER FIVE

The Restoration Period: Dryden and Halifax. The Lesson for Today

(i)

THERE is a story of a man 'who having been given a copy of Dr Johnson's Dictionary to read, did so faithfully, and observed at the conclusion that the Author was an excellent writer, but not at all "connected" '.* If the application of this anecdote is not immediately apparent, it will, I am afraid, become so in the course of the remarks I have now to make, which, starting from some observations on two or three writers of the later seventeenth century, will proceed by an irregular course to those matters of immediate and topical interest with which the series began. But at the end I will make explicit the few simple things I have been trying to say, hoping that from my small dictionary of quotations an intelligible and useful sentence may emerge.

A full study of the political literature of the post-Restoration period (excluding the political philosophers such as Hobbes and Locke) might well begin with Butler's *Hudibras*, which demands a passing tribute here if only because in it Butler suggests a connexion between the way men talk and the way they act.

> When *civil* Fury first grew high,
> And men fell out they knew not why;
> When hard words, *Jealousies* and *Fears*,

* I take the anecdote from a note in Grosart's edition of Marvell's *Works*, Vol. IV, p. 426.

Set Folks together by the ears,
And made them fight, like mad or drunk,
For Dame *Religion* as for Punk,
Whose honesty they all durst swear for,
Though not a man of them knew wherefore:
When *Gospel-trumpeter*, surrounded
With long-ear'd rout, to Battel sounded,
And Pulpit, Drum Ecclesiastick,
Was beat with fist, instead of a stick:
Then did Sir *Knight* abandon dwelling,
And out he rode a Colonelling.

The prejudice is obvious; but in the lines,

When hard words, *Jealousies* and *Fears*,
Set Folks together by the ears,

there is an important grain of truth. Dr John Wilders, in his edition of the poem, points out that 'hard words' means both harsh words and cant words, used by the Puritans, of which 'jealousies' (suspicions) and 'fears' are examples.* 'Hard words' are clichés or party slogans, unexamined generalities carrying a strong emotional charge, so that they quickly become hard words in another sense: they can literally knock you down. The resulting state of affairs, as depicted in the poem, is in turn supported by a further misuse of language

For he was of that stubborn Crew
Of Errant Saints, whom all men grant
To be the true Church *Militant*:
Such as do build their Faith upon
The holy Text of *Pike* and *Gun*;

* Samuel Butler, *Hudibras*, edited with an Introduction by John Wilders (Oxford English Texts), p. 322. Dr Wilders aptly quotes from Hobbes, *Leviathan*, II, xxix: 'When the spiritual power moveth the members of a commonwealth . . . and by strange, and hard words suffocates their understanding, it must needs distract the people, and either overwhelm the commonwealth with oppression, or cast it into the fire of a civil war'.

> Decide all Controversies by
> Infallible *Artillery*;
> And prove their Doctrine Orthodox
> By Apostolick *Blows* and *Knocks*;
> Call Fire and Sword and Desolation,
> A *godly-thorough-Reformation*.*

Obviously we can't make too much of this, and I am not now concerned with the justice of Butler's picture of Presbyterian and Sectary. In an age of consolidation and reorganization following a great upheaval the events of the immediate past are only too likely to be distorted, and we certainly don't go to Butler for an understanding of puritanism and the civil war. It is enough if we keep in mind his suggestion of the potentially explosive force of words.

In the literature of the post-Restoration period Dryden is *the* representative voice of the conservative establishment. One would have to be very dim-witted not to enjoy Dryden's satires. It is a matter of common experience that once they have been read, lines and passages can't be dislodged from the memory, and this—though not an infallible test—is a presumption that we have been listening to a distinctive individual voice. It is largely a matter of tone and movement, as we see when lines are read aloud with the modulation and emphasis they demand:

> During his office, treason was no crime,
> The sons of Belial had a glorious time.

---

* Compare:

> And therefore being inform'd by bruit,
> That *Dog* and *Bear* are to dispute;
> For so of late man fighting name,
> Because they often prove the same;
> (For where the first does hap to be,
> The last does *coincidere*) . . .

96

The midwife laid her hand on his thick skull,
With this prophetic blessing,—*Be thou dull*.

To die for faction is a common evil,
But to be hanged for nonsense is the devil.

Almighty crowd! thou shortenest all dispute,
Power is thy essence, wit thy attribute!
Nor faith nor reason make thee at a stay,
Thou leapst o'er all eternal truths in thy Pindaric way!

Since his rehabilitation after the period of Arnoldian dis-
favour Dryden's merits have been sufficiently recognized.
What also has to be recognized is that when Dryden speaks
with a public voice—and it is only infrequently, as in the
lines 'To the Memory of Mr Oldham', that he does not
speak with a public voice—his strength works within rather
narrow bounds. His limitations are of a kind that prevents
him from offering intellectual nourishment to those of later
generations who may turn to him with their own problems
of public order or disorder in mind; and I think they are
determined by the complete absence from his verse of
what I have referred to as resonance and perspective.

There is no need, for example, to doubt the sincerity
of his religious convictions, whether before or after his
conversion to Roman Catholicism; but there is surely a
lack of resonance in his jaunty or complacent use of
religious analogies for secular purposes. There are
examples in *The Medal*; and in a Prologue addressed to
the Duke of York 'upon his first appearance at the Duke's
Theatre since his return from Scotland' (where he had
prudently resided during most of the exclusion controversy), there is surely something odd when the angels are
seen as making 'their solemn show at Heaven's White-
hall', just as there is something excessive in the reference
to the heir presumptive—

Thus angels on glad messages appear;
Their first salute commands us not to fear.

The effect is similar when the analogies work the other
way.

To take up half on trust and half to try,
Name it not faith, but bungling bigotry.
Both knave and fool the merchant we may call
To pay great sums and to compound the small,
For who would break with Heaven, and would not break
for all?
Rest then, my soul, from endless anguish freed:
Nor sciences thy guide, nor sense thy creed.
Faith is the best insurer of thy bliss;
The bank above must fail before the venture miss.

To speak of a lack of resonance, then, is to refer to the
absence of some essential quality or awareness that, given
the matter under discussion, we feel instinctively ought
to be there. And this is so, I think, in the vigorous satires
of 1681 and 1682, directed against Shaftesbury and the
Whigs, that were Dryden's contribution to the great
national debate of those years. In the brutal confusion of
the so-called Popish Plot and the exclusion crisis—and
for an understanding of *Absalom and Achitophel*, *The
Medal* and *MacFlecknoe* we need to inform ourselves on
these matters—Dryden certainly had a function. As
Professor Ogg says, 'There are times in history when
national sanity can be restored only by sarcasm. . . . It
was so . . . in England when, after three years of madness,
men read *Absalom and Achitophel* and laughed themselves
out of their follies. It was the triumph of native common
sense.'* This may well have been the case; but so far as

* David Ogg, *England in the Reign of Charles II* (O.U.P. paperback edition,
1967), pp. 630-1.

98

the perennial value of the poem is concerned, it was a triumph achieved at some cost. Not only is the argument less clear and sure than the tone seems to assert, there is a complete absence of shading. No one has ever been so funny about his political and personal opponents—but at the cost of a constant refusal to see them as anything but distorted two-dimensional figures. 'I must confess', said Dryden, in one of those bantering remarks that make one like him, 'I am no great artist; but sign-post painting will serve the turn to remember a friend by, especially when better is not to be had' (*The Medal*, prefatory 'Epistle to the Whigs'). Sign-post paintings—with their crudity of colour and disregard for exact verisimilitude—is what most of his character-sketches are.

> A martial hero first, with early care
> Blown, like a pigmy by the winds, to war;
> A beardless chief, a rebel ere a man,
> So young his hatred to his Prince began.
> Next this, (how wildly will ambition steer!)
> A vermin wriggling in the usurper's ear,
> Bartering his venal wit for sums of gold,
> He cast himself into the saint-like mould;
> Groaned, sighed, and prayed, while godliness was gain,
> The loudest bag-pipe of the squeaking train.
> But, as 'tis hard to cheat a juggler's eyes,
> His open lewdness he could ne'er disguise.
> There split the saint; for hypocritic zeal
> Allows no sins but those it can conceal.

Much of this, as a portrait of Shaftesbury, simply is not true.* Nor was the later rule of Charles II when freed from the embarrassment of a Parliament, for which Dryden had helped pave the way, a happy comment on the

---

* Leaving aside the fact that both here, in *The Medal*, and in the earlier portrait in *Absalom and Achitophel*, Dryden blames Shaftesbury for attitudes and acts which he himself had earlier approved.

sweeping arguments put forward in *Absalom and Achitophel*
against any kind of opposition to the King.*

> Not only crowds but Sanhedrins may be
> Infected with this public lunacy,
> And share the madness of rebellious times,
> To murder monarchs for imagined crimes.
> If they may give and take whene'er they please,
> Not kings alone, the Godhead's images,
> But government itself at length must fall
> To nature's state, where all have right to all.
> Yet grant our lords, the people, kings can make,
> What prudent men a settled throne would shake?
> For whatsoe'er their sufferings were before,
> The change they covet makes them suffer more.
> All other errors but disturb a state,
> But innovation is the blow of fate.
> If ancient fabrics nod and threat to fall,
> To patch the flaws and buttress up the wall,
> Thus far 'tis duty: but here fix the mark;
> For all beyond it is to touch our ark.
> To change foundations, cast the frame anew,
> Is work for rebels who base ends pursue,
> At once divine and human laws control,
> And mend the parts by ruin of the whole.
> The tampering world is subject to this curse,
> To physic their disease into a worse.

The tenor of the argument, with its begged questions, the
tone and imagery—the building metaphors so different
from Marvell's in 'The Second Anniversary'—suggest
the limitations of Dryden's conservatism. Here, and in
The Medal, he sees no third way between a Hobbesian
and unqualified acceptance of the *status quo* and 'anarchy'.
His political position allows no room for manœuvre, just
as his style carries the reader to an unquestioning acceptance of his one-sided case, where all the arguing is done

* See Ogg, *op. cit.*, Chapter vii, 'The Stuart Revenge: 1681-5'.

in terms of contemptuous caricature.[23] His satire has none of the positive feeling for what is attacked that we find so often in Pope; he lacks Pope's larger historical sense,* and Pope's justified conviction that what he is defending are the precarious values, not of a particular social establishment, but of civilization.

It has been said of *Absalom and Achitophel* that in it,

> Dryden now displays the full intellectual and literary resources of his time. The less he has to invent the better, for the poem must seem a reassuring summary of belief and feeling given in such a way as to confirm beyond any further question the truth of what it says. It has to raise the great issues of all societies and answer them finally.†

The first two sentences are fair comment (though I should question the word 'intellectual'); but if the third is meant to indicate what Dryden achieved rather than what he may have intended, it is, I think, wrong. Scorn and contempt erect too many barriers for the poet to achieve that kind of universality. The political poems compel our admiration for the vigorous use of 'the naked thew and sinew of the English language',‡ but they have not the seminal power of the imagination in politics that can inform and nourish the thoughts of men in later ages when they address themselves to 'the great issues of all societies'.

---

* On which, see Howard Erskine-Hill, 'Augustans on Augustanism: England, 1655-1759', *Renaissance and Modern Studies*, Vol. XI, 1967, and 'The Medal against Time: a Study of Pope's epistle *To Mr Addison*', *Journal of the Warburg and Courtauld Institutes*, Vol. XXVIII, 1965.

† Bernard N. Schilling, *Dryden and the Conservative Myth*, p. 135. 'The poem goes beyond its occasion and penetrates to the elements inseparable from the human condition and the way in which its affairs must be governed' (p. 139). The book has, however, many valuable things to say about Dryden and his age, including some discussion of the element of fear in the Conservative temper.

‡ *The Letters of Gerard Manley Hopkins to Robert Bridges*, ed. Claude Colleer Abbott, pp. 267-8.

In the later seventeenth century there is only one public voice that in some important respects can be compared with Marvell's: it is the voice of George Savile, Marquess of Halifax—the Trimmer. I have neither time nor ability to describe the part played by Halifax in the political life of three reigns, and I mention him here only to call attention to the *way* in which he conducts a political argument in two of his best known works, *The Character of a Trimmer* and *A Letter to a Dissenter*—a style which is so much more than mere style. Halifax's wit and easy clarity are known to all who have looked at the famous *Character of King Charles II*. The political writings are witty and clear, but the wit and clarity are not only vehicles for what could be conveyed by other means: they are part of the temper that informs the substance, and is, so to speak, one with it.

> No man doth less approve the ill-bred Methods of some of the Dissenters, in rebuking Authority, who behave themselves as if they thought ill manners necessary to Salvation: yet he cannot but distinguish and desire a Mean between the sawcyness of some of the *Scotch Apostles*, and the undecent Courtship of some of the Silken Divines, who, one would think, do practice to bow at the Altar, only to learn to make the better Legs at Court.*

It seems a trivial observation to say that this piece of well-bred contempt for two extremes balances on a 'yet'. But it hasn't, I think, been sufficiently observed how Halifax's style, in *The Character of a Trimmer*, is determined by the constant use of qualifiers, such as 'though', 'yet' and 'on the other side', and explanatory connectives such as 'for'. The summary of his constitutional position hinges on the little word 'yet'.

* Halifax, *Complete Works*, edited with an Introduction by Walter Raleigh, p. 74.

Our Trimmer . . . professeth solemnly that were it in his Power to chuse, he would rather have his Ambition bounded by the Commands of a Great and Wise Master, than let it range with a Popular Licence, tho' crown'd with success: yet he cannot commit such a Sin against the glorious thing called Liberty, nor let his Soul stoop so much below itself, as to be content without repining to have his Reason wholly subdu'd, or the Privilege of Acting like a sensible Creature torn from him by the imperious Dictates of unlimited Authority, in what hand so ever it happens to be plac'd.*

Halifax's appeal to 'Prudence, Humanity and Common Sense' lacks Marvell's awareness of the potentially tragic nature of conflict; but he shares with him a sense of the folly of going against the grain of history, the sense that 'permanence'—in Coleridge's terms—must be balanced against 'progression'. Sometimes it is necessary, as he advised the Dissenters, simply to wait on the times.† It is of course this larger awareness that puts him apart from the simplifiers. In an age when public insanity and panic fear seemed endemic,‡ he was able, when dealing with immediate issues, to use a public voice that still speaks to us.

Amongst all the Engines of Dissention, there hath been none more powerful in all Times, than the fixing Names upon one another of Contumely and Reproach. . . . But 'tis hard, that men will not only invent ill Names, but they will wrest and misinterpret good ones; so afraid some are even of a reconciling sound, that they raise another noise to keep it from being heard, lest it should set up and encourage a dangerous sort of Men, who prefer Peace and Agreement, before Violence and Confusion.

This translates easily into our own idiom. It may not be

* *Op. cit.*, p. 100.
† See the concluding paragraphs of the *Letter to a Dissenter*.
‡ See Ogg, *op. cit.*, pp. 594-5, 612.

strictly true that, as a modern writer puts it, 'to have enemies we need labels',* but they are a great help. At all times name-calling, the attachment of labels—Zealot, Puritan, Jacobin, Commie, Agitator, Bourgeois, the Establishment, Pig, Hippy, etc.—gives a semblance of objective form to our projections, thereby strengthening the fears from which they spring, and diminishing our chances of dealing creatively with the material offered us by our present. The virtue of Halifax's style is that it is one in which it is impossible to create bogies.†

(ii)

I am not sure how much further we should pursue the speculations to which I have invited you in these lectures —or how far I am capable of pursuing them. Most of the material I have offered has been drawn from writings of the English 'century of revolution'; and perhaps the best way of returning to our starting-point is to consider briefly the larger questions of radical change in public life. It may sometimes seem that the armed and violent phase of all the classic revolutions of modern times have resulted in a state of affairs towards which the strongest pressures in society were working *before* the revolution, and which would in all probability have come about without the revolutionary recourse to violence. It has, for example, been said of the English revolution that

* Gordon W. Allport, *The Nature of Prejudice* (Doubleday Anchor Books), p. 179.

† Jeremy Taylor had noted the part played by fear in promoting a zealous contentiousness: '. . . in things men understand not, they are most impetuous; and because suspicion is a thing infinite in degrees, for it hath nothing to determine it,—a suspicious person is ever most violent; for his fears are worse than the thing feared, because the thing is limited, but his fears are not'.—*Liberty of Prophesying, Works* (1880). Vol. II, p. 319.

'through political change and upheaval the social order remained unshaken at its foundations, emerging intact in the aftermath of the cataclysm on the same continuum along which it had been evolving before'.[24] The absorption into the constitutional process of a class of men with interests, outlooks and abilities different from those of the Tudor and early-Stuart court-centred administration may perhaps have been accelerated, but at the cost of great violence and great suffering, which, with its legacy of bitterness and fear made a *negative* contribution to public life in the years that followed.[25] To say this is not to deny the value of the ideals expressed by some of the more radical figures of the time (for example, the Levellers); just as, at a later period, the words in which Blake and Wordsworth evoked what they thought they saw in the early phases of the French Revolution are permanent reminders of central human needs. It is simply to raise the question of whether men are capable of making radical change in society, where it needs to be made, without the appeal to mass passions that are not always related to particular forms of injustice and particular remedies, but that *are* likely to ally themselves with hatreds and hysterias decidedly unfriendly to the ends ostensibly proposed. The question really is whether any revolution has been revolutionary enough, whether it has done anything to break the patterns of domination which both public and private life have inherited from the past.*

It seems to me that, as the twentieth century slowly approaches the twenty-first, this is an absolutely fundamental question for all who are concerned with what the

---

* See D. W. Harding, *The Impulse to Dominate*. Patterns of domination are of course transmitted and reinforced by an idiom of physical and moral assault that protesting groups find it only too easy to take over.

future may bring. It is a very large question, demanding the attention of minds of the first order, possessing well grounded and wide-ranging historical imagination, as well as alertness to, and concern for, the present; and the questions I have raised, if certainly not small, come within the capacities of ordinary people like teachers of English. An attempt to relate them, and so to bring us back to our starting-point, must form my concluding section.

In a contribution to the *Courier* (Dec. 21, 1809), Coleridge remarked that 'the error, which of all others is the most tremendous in its consequences, is an inward prostration of the soul before enormous POWER'.* The core of his objection to the violent phase of the French Revolution was that it led—inevitably led—to this prostration. In *The Friend*, and elsewhere,† he makes what is, I suppose, a classic case against 'the politics of pure reason', which, instead of a prudent handling of particular situations in the light of universal principles, attempts to strait-jacket human diversity with laws as abstract and inflexible as those of geometry. Coleridge's arguments against 'Jacobinism' demand to be read in full. They are the more effective because he was not a mere anti-Jacobin[26]: his aim was not denunciation but understanding. But his warnings are still valid: the triumph of a party claiming a mathematical certainty for its own programme—and therefore representing the will of the people if only the people knew their own minds— leads inevitably to tyranny (an 'ever-neighbouring control', he called it in a *Courier* essay, with an eye on the

* *Essays on his own Times*, ed. Sarah Coleridge (1850), Vol. II, p. 645.

† See especially *The Friend*, ed. Barbara Rooke, Vol. I, pp. 163 ff. ('Section the First: on the Principles of Political Knowledge'), and *The Statesman's Manual*, in *Political Tracts of Wordsworth, Coleridge, Shelley*, ed. R. J. White, pp. 27-28 and *passim*.

dictator's police state),* in which the true meaning of a state—a body politic composed of individual members with their own personal and inter-personal needs—would be sacrificed to an abstraction.

> Now this contains the sublime philosophy of the sect of Economists [sc. physiocrats]. They worship a kind of non-entity under the different words, the State, the Whole, the Society, &c. and to this idol they make bloodier sacrifices than ever the Mexicans did to Tescalipoca.†

But Coleridge does not only warn against the ruthless application of 'legislative geometry' by men who believe they have a blueprint for human happiness. His positive contribution to political thinking is threefold. (*a*) He reminds us that the state is in fact a society of persons, and that to get full recognition for the necessary interdependence of its members is as much a necessity in our thinking about the state as it is in our thinking about *all* social groups. What he calls 'the actual immanence of all in each'‡ is as relevant to politics as—it is now beginning to be recognized—it is to psychiatry.§ As he says in the *Essay on Faith*: 'Each man in a numerous society is not only co-existent with, but virtually organised into

* 'Shut up in a labyrinthine prison of forms and bye-laws, of engagements by oath and contributions by compulsion, they move in slavish files beneath a jealous and ever-neighbouring control, which despotises in detail; in which every man is made his brother's keeper; and which arming the hand and fixing the eye of all against each, merges the free-will of the individual in the merciless tyranny of the confederation.'—*Essays on his own Times* (1850), Vol. III, p. 694.

† Compare Trotsky: 'The Jacobins spared no human hecatomb to build the pedestal for their Truth. . . . The counterpart to their absolute faith in a metaphysical idea was their absolute distrust of living people.'—Quoted by Isaac Deutscher, *The Prophet Armed. Trotsky: 1879-1925*, p. 91.

‡ *The Statesman's Manual*, in White, *op. cit.*, pp. 28-9.

§ R. D. Laing's *The Divided Self* is perhaps the best known exposition of this.

the multitude of which he is an integral part. His *idem* is modified by the *alter*, myself and my neighbour'; and, 'there can be no I without a Thou'. (*b*) He reminds us that the political temper of an age cannot be separated from its prevailing intellectual and moral temper, the nature and direction of its tastes and interests. And (*c*) he reminds us that the collective mind of a people is embodied in a language. Only language rooted in the imagination can keep men from 'the hollowness of abstractions'; only language used with the degree of precision proper to its subject can keep thought vigorously alive. In the *Biographia Literaria* he speaks of 'a debility and deadness of the imaginative power', which renders the mind liable to superstition and fanaticism, and of 'the beneficial after-effects of verbal precision in the preclusion of fanaticism, which masters the feelings more especially by indistinct watch-words'. 'Party rage, and fanatical aversion,' he says elsewhere, 'have their birthplace and natural abode in floating and obscure generalities, and seldom or never burst forth, except from clouds and vapours.'[27] To learn from Coleridge is to learn not to be dominated by absolutist political claims, to learn what can, and what cannot, properly be expected from political speech and action; it is to learn something about the relation between language and statesmanship.

Now this, you may say, is all very well, but it has little to do with the hard facts of political life; it cannot be translated into terms that relate directly to what is done in politics as they are conducted here and not in Utopia. I am not so sure. I am largely ignorant of American history, but I should like to propose for consideration the case of Abraham Lincoln. Lincoln's public style is not easy to describe. Grave and weighty, capable of a plain but rigorous logic in the analysis of tangled circumstances, its staple is a simple and direct speech, shot through with homely idiom—'This is as plain as adding up the weight of three small hogs', 'The plainest point cannot be read through a gold eagle', '. . . a specious and fantastic arrangement of words, by which a man can prove a horse chestnut to be a chestnut horse'. These are not added piquancies; they express a sense of the pressure of a real world on the statesman's policies, and they go with Lincoln's grasp of relevant facts in a complex situation. (Abstraction he referred to as 'merely pernicious'.) In other words, he was aware of complications that couldn't simply be wished away; but the long sentences that hold this awareness before his audience alternate with short and direct statements that show clearly where he has come out.

> What has been said of Louisiana [regarding its interim constitution at the end of the Civil War] will apply generally to other States. And yet so great peculiarities pertain to each state; and such important and sudden changes occur in the same state; and, withal, so new and unprecedented is the whole case, that no exclusive, and inflexible plan can safely be prescribed as to details and collaterals. Such exclusive, and inflexible plan, would surely become a new entanglement. Important principles may, and must, be inflexible.

To firmness of principle and flexibility of application, we have to add other qualities: the rejection of a self-righteous attitude of total condemnation of those whom he stubbornly opposed—'With malice towards none' is the keynote of his second Inaugural*; the non-divisive manner of a way of speech that seeks to be heard across formidable

---

* He hated slavery, but as Dr J. R. Pole has said, 'He had never blamed the slave-owners for their historical predicament, and never having blamed them he felt no desire to punish them'. *Abraham Lincoln and the American Commitment* (a Centenary Lecture delivered in the University of Cambridge, 1965), p. 36.

barriers—'I do not argue. I beseech you to make the
arguments for yourselves. You can not, if you would, be
blind to the signs of the times.' And finally there is again
and again the opening up to the perspectives of history,
a sense of the place of the present moment in a continuous
process greater than one man can grasp. Characteristic
openings are:

> If we could first know *where* we are, and *whither* we are
> tending, we could then better judge *what* to do, and *how* to
> do it . . .

> Four score and seven years ago our fathers brought forth on
> this continent, a new nation, conceived in Liberty, and dedi-
> cated to the proposition that all men are created equal.

> It has long been a grave question whether any government,
> not *too* strong for the liberties of its people, can be strong
> *enough* to maintain its own existence, in great emergencies.

An American historian quotes from one of the most
famous of Lincoln's speeches when seeking election to
the Senate, ' "A house divided against itself cannot
stand", I believe this government cannot endure, per-
manently half *slave* and half *free*', and comments:

> This might be considered revolutionary doctrine if it were
> not for the insertion of the word 'permanently', which lends
> special emphasis to the fact that the speaker was scanning a
> distant horizon, not just the proximate ground of sectional
> controversy.*

The qualification does not imply any shilly-shallying
about what Lincoln early called 'the monstrous injustice
of slavery'; it means merely, in Carl Sandburg's words,
that 'he could relate the tangled past to the uncertain
future by offering only what might be workable in the

* Don E. Fehrenbacher, *Prelude to Greatness: Lincoln in the 1850s*, p. 75.

immediate present'*; but the horizons of past and future were always before him as he spoke. He was capable of firm and decisive action; but he was also aware of what time alone could do. 'I claim not to have controlled events,' he said, 'but confess plainly that events have controlled me.' It may well be true also, as Dr Pole drily comments, that 'there had at least been a fair measure of give-and-take between Lincoln and the events that controlled him',† but his waiting on events was very much more than mere political shrewdness: it was part of his hope—bitterly frustrated though it was—that men *might* spare their pains when nature was at work. And I suspect, though I cannot prove, that there is a connexion between Lincoln's wide perspectives and the actuality and resonance of his style, which sometimes rises to a strange eloquence. Time and repetition have not staled the Gettysburg address; here, as elsewhere, the style is the magnanimity of the man, and as much as any decision taken or action performed it is part of his politics.‡

But it is time to return from this poaching expedition and to draw towards an end. In that remarkable book, *The Rebel*,§ Camus distinguishes between 'revolt', which is always necessary, and 'revolution', which in claiming universality erects its own tyranny. In our time, he says (the book appeared in 1951), 'Dialogue and personal relations have been replaced by propaganda or polemic, which are two kinds of monologue. Abstraction, which belongs to the world of power and calculation, has replaced

* Carl Sandburg, *Abraham Lincoln* (Laurel Edition), Vol. I, p. 178.

† J. R. Pole, *op. cit.*, p. 5.

‡ All quotations in the last two paragraphs are from *Abraham Lincoln: a Documentary Portrait through his Speeches and Writings*, edited with an Introduction by Don E. Fehrenbacher (Signet Classics).

§ Albert Camus, *L'homme révolté*, translated by Anthony Bower (Penguin Books).

the real passions . . . love and friendship submitted
to a doctrine and destiny to a plan.' Revolt, on the other
hand, is the friend of moderation, *mesure*, which implies
that you take your stand on this or this particular issue,
whilst still accepting the complexities of the public no
less than of the private life. '*La mesure . . . est une pure
tension.*' With this in mind we can return to the question
of political language and the relation between language
and action. In my first lecture I spoke of some of the
dangers that we need to be fully conscious of in various
forms of public speech. There is the danger of a public
language so imprecise that nothing can be firmly grasped
or clearly focused. There is the danger of various kinds
of totalitarian ideology, using a 'closed' language that,
as Roland Barthes said of Stalinist writing, 'aims at presenting reality in a prejudged form'.[28] And, sharing the
vices of both kinds, there is the language of bureaucratic
control and of the mass persuaders. Faced with such
dangers we can perhaps see why it is of such vital importance that, even as political men, we should be familiar
with and keep alive the language of the imagination—a
language capable of grasping the actual in its human
variety and complexity, and that invites us to questioning
and dialogue; for it is only through questioning and openness to experience that we can clarify our values and make
our responsible choices in the political—as in any other
—sphere. 'To organize a new union between our political
ideas and our imagination', says Lionel Trilling, '—in all
our cultural purview there is no work more necessary.'*
Poets, of course, are not in any precise sense the unack-
nowledged legislators of the world; statesmen and legislators are not—or not usually—poets, and we do not

---

* Lionel Trilling, 'The Function of the Little Magazine', *The Liberal
Imagination*, p. 100. The whole essay is relevant to the present discussion.

expect them to use the language of poetry. What we may hope and work for—though not necessarily expect—is that there should not be a *complete* divorce between the language of those who handle our public affairs and the language that expresses the deepest truths of our nature. A healthy public language, even when used to express passionate conviction, is always 'open': it *looks towards* the life of reason and imagination, and, whatever its ostensible drive, implicitly reminds us that values only exist in the personal and extra-political. Teachers of literature do the state some service when they help others to see how great writers bring politics into relation with humanity and intelligence, and, by their very handling of language, offer to those who are willing to learn a new organ of thought for dealing effectively with matters of shared concern. The truth about public matters cannot be spoken in a merely public voice; and for those of us who 'teach the humanities' to get *that* recognized is perhaps our most useful—though it need not be our only—contribution to the political life of our time.

Notes

1 (see page 13)

Blake, *Works*, ed. Keynes (Nonesuch, 1957), p. 600. It should be noticed that the next page of the Note-book begins: 'The wretched state of the Arts in this Country and in Europe, originating in the wretched state of Political Science, which is the Science of Sciences . . .'; and Blake goes on to talk about the way in which the arts have been made into instruments of political aggrandizement. There is of course no contradiction. Blake is making a distinction between politics—the jobbing and speechifying at Westminster—and political science; and we can agree with him that political science, the knowledge of how men ought to live together in the polis, is in some sense 'the science of sciences'.

2 (see page 17)

We touch here on the vital link between politics and basic education in a more than minimal literacy. An American writer, Mr John Wilkinson, with experience as a university teacher, states that a test given in six American colleges and universities showed that more than 90 per cent of the students had, as freshmen, 'a usable active vocabulary of about 800 words', and that there was 'a 20 per cent *decrease* in these numbers during the four-year passage from freshman to senior'. He adds:

I have no objective measurements, but a very strong subjective impression, that ten years after graduation the vocabulary of these students is even smaller. This intuition is confirmed by analyses of the vocabularies used in the mass media. It would be fatuous indeed, therefore, to suppose that the great majority of Americans are in a position to deliberate upon political or other issues for which they have no words.

Mr Wilkinson quotes Robert M. Hutchins: 'With an educational system that does not educate and a system of mass communication that does not communicate, we have become incapable of the discussion by which political issues are determined'.*

I have no means of checking the—almost incredible—figures quoted above. Whatever the exact size of the average vocabulary of any representative group of American college students (and enlargement is not encouraged by some so-called radical journalism I have seen), the danger of a language apparently intended for the almost illiterate is real enough. If anyone thinks that it is confined to the United States he should look up some of the speeches delivered in the summer of 1970 immediately before the General Election. Mr Wilson (after speaking of the improvement in the economy):

> And there is a feeling of liberation, of a loosening of constriction on personal initiative, of a freedom of individual choice, combined with a national system of order and stability which makes us the envy of every civilized country. . . . This is responsible government. . . . Against this we have to set the record in opposition of the Conservative Party. . ., a record of unremitting irresponsibility, social irresponsibility, economic irresponsibility, in government and opposition alike.

Mr Heath (on the record of the Labour Government):

> The last five years show that this Labour Government will only do what they are forced into by events or by what is politically necessary to save themselves. All they think about is their short-term party interests. . . . Look where it has got them: the mere plaything of events: just the pathetic wreckage of what a British Government should be. Everybody knows they are a soft touch, a pushover. They are men of straw. They bend to every wind. Like cushions, they merely bear the imprint of the last person who sat on them.

No one would judge either Mr Wilson or Mr Heath on the evidence of a few sentences in election speeches. But they were,

* See John Wilkinson, 'The Civilization of the Dialogue', in *The Dissenting Academy*, ed. Theodore Roszak (New York: Vintage Books, 1968; London: Chatto and Windus, 1969), pp. 173-7.

after all, speaking on an occasion that demanded something other than dis-incentives to thought, and one can only agree with *The Times'* Political Correspondent, Mr David Wood, that 'any serious but uncommitted voter who studied the leaders' speeches in the hope of forming his judgment for June 18 would brush aside both texts in despair'.* A further quotation from Mr Wood is in order here:

> Mr Wilson and Mr Heath [in their election speeches] were anti-stylists, and will go on being anti-stylist, because they deliver their speeches to one small audience in the hope of catching the ear and the eye of quite another audience . . . the millions of television viewers and the skimmers of tomorrow's newspapers. . . . The contemporary party leader's speech is much made up of verbless slogans, and the adjectives, if any, are all sound and fury, like 'massive', signifying nothing in particular. The slogans are machine-turned to be fired off staccato into a microphone. . . . So far as this may be reckoned a style of political speech at all, I suspect it to be a style that is unfriendly to truth and alien to anything that deserves to be called reason; and in so far as style grows out of the essence of the man, one inseparable from the other, I wish to say that I do not think so ill of Mr Wilson or Mr Heath as to believe that they can practise a spurious style without becoming themselves spurious. †

It is true that England has not yet developed the full American TV technique for 'selling' political leaders like detergents and breakfast foods, as described in a horror-story by Mr Joe McGinnis, *The Selling of the President*.‡ But we are catching up. Ten months before the Election the *Sunday Times* informed its readers:

> Labour Party leaders today launch a £200,000 pre-election advertising and publicity campaign with 'Soul' as its theme. 'Labour's got life *and* soul' is the slogan in full-page newspaper advertisements. Lapel badges distributed to party workers and M.P.'s will proclaim 'I'm a soul mate, mate!' 'Let's go

---

* Quotations and comment from *The Times*, May 30, 1970.
† 'Shrieking to be Heard', *The Times*, June 1, 1970.
‡ André Deutsch and Penguin Books, 1970.

with life and soul', 'I'm the life and soul of the party' or, simply, 'Soul!'. . . This first phase of the campaign, which Transport House calls 'the big bang', will last a month, culminating in the Brighton Party conference. 'We want the electors to start thinking about the fundamentals of politics', explained Mr Gwyn Morgan, the Party's assistant general secretary.*

After the public show ('What were we doing on such a day?') presumably Mr Heath and the rest got back to the real work of which they are capable. I am not now discussing their respective abilities. The point is that this is an age in which it is increasingly difficult to master the facts and assess the values involved in any major public decision, whether in economic policy or with regard to the siting of a new airport. The use of election catch-phrases like 'Now Britain is strong, let's make it great to live in', where one senses the hotched-up enthusiasm of the television advertiser, does *nothing* to educate the electorate. The spread of such methods will mean the death of democracy as traditionally understood.

3 (see page 18)
Some further examples are given by Theodore Roszak in *The Making of a Counter Culture* in a passage that deserves to be quoted in full.

When knowledgeable men talk, they no longer talk of substances and accidents, of being and spirit, of virtue and vice, of sin and salvation, of deities and demons. Instead, we have a vocabulary filled with nebulous quantities of things that have every appearance of precise calibration, and decorated with vaguely mechanistic-mathematical terms like 'parameters', 'structures', 'variables', 'inputs and outputs', 'correlations', 'inventories', 'maximizations', and 'optimizations'. The terminology derives from involuted statistical procedures and methodological mysteries to which only graduate education gives access. The more such language and numerology one packs into a document, the more 'objective' the document becomes—which normally means the less morally abrasive to

* The *Sunday Times*, August 31, 1969.

the sources that have subsidized the research or to any sources that might conceivably subsidize one's research at any time in the future. The vocabulary and the methodology mask the root ethical assumptions of policy or neatly transcribe them into a depersonalized rhetoric which provides a gloss of military or political necessity. To think and to talk in such terms becomes the sure sign of being a certified realist, a 'hard research' man.

Thus to bomb more hell out of a tiny Asian country in one year than was bombed out of Europe in the whole Second World War becomes 'escalation'. Threatening to burn and blast to death several million civilians in an enemy country is called 'deterrence'. Turning a city into radioactive rubble is called 'taking out' a city. A concentration camp (already a euphemism for a political prison) becomes a 'strategic hamlet'. A comparison of the slaughter on both sides in a war is called a 'kill ratio'. Totalling up the corpses is called a 'body count'. Running the blacks out of town is called 'urban renewal'. Discovering ingenious new ways to bilk the public is called 'market research'. Outflanking the discontent of employees is called 'personnel management'. Wherever possible, hideous realities are referred to by cryptic initials and formulalike phrases: ICBM, CBR, megadeaths, or 'operation' this, 'operation' that. On the other hand, one can be certain that where more colorful, emotive terms are used—'the war on poverty', 'the war for the hearts and minds of men', 'the race for space', 'the New Frontier', 'the Great Society'—the matters referred to exist only as propagandistic fictions or pure distraction.*

There may be some exaggeration here, but it is the uncomfortable truth rather than a few rhetorical exaggerations that we should attend to: the examples are of course American, but these things have an easy Transatlantic crossing.

4 (see page 25)
See Charles Parkin, *The Moral Basis of Burke's Political Thought,*

* Theodore Roszak, *The Making of a Counter Culture* (Anchor Books; Doubleday and Company Inc.), pp. 142-4. Quoted by permission of the publishers.

a book to which I am greatly indebted. Like Coleridge, who learnt from him, Burke will allow no short-cuts to political wisdom: it is only when we fully engage with the intractable that we learn what we are really dealing with. 'Difficulty is a severe instructor . . . *Pater ipse colendi haud facilem esse viam voluit.* He that wrestles with us strengthens our nerves, and sharpens our skill. Our antagonist is our helper. This amicable conflict with difficulty obliges us to an intimate acquaintance with our object, and compels us to consider it in all its relations. It will not suffer us to be superficial. It is the want of nerves of understanding for such a task; it is the degenerate fondness for tricking short-cuts . . . that has in so many parts of the world created governments with arbitrary powers.'— *Reflections*, ed. Conor Cruise O'Brien (Penguin), pp. 278-9.

5 (see page 26)

James T. Boulton, *The Language of Politics in the Age of Wilkes and Burke* (Routledge and Kegan Paul, 1963), p. 98. This in many ways pioneering book deserves to be widely known. With its central conviction, 'that the insights obtained from a literary-critical examination of . . . political writings should be considered by historians and political theorists as significant to their own special enquiries', I am of course in complete agreement. Where I find myself in disagreement is with what appears to be the assumption that literary analysis of the devices of political writing can be divorced from evaluation. Later (p. 122) Dr Boulton admits that Burke sometimes allows himself to 'exploit emotionalism of a specious kind'.

6 (see page 29)

George Digby, Second Earl of Bristol—described by Horace Walpole as 'a singular person, whose life was one contradiction' (*D.N.B.*)—is said by Gardiner to have been won over by the smiles of Henrietta Maria. Clarendon, who had been intimate with him, gives an interesting account of his accomplishments and weaknesses.* In the trial of Strafford the prosecution was on slippery ground. None of Strafford's actions, taken singly, however high-

* S. R. Gardiner, *History of England, 1603-42*, Vol. IX, pp. 338-9. The character of Digby in Clarendon's *History of the Rebellion* is included in the *Selections from Clarendon*, ed. G. Huehns (World's Classics), pp. 186-90.

handed, could be defined as treason. So it was claimed that 'cumulatively' they amounted to treason. The only words that could be construed as treasonable, as the law then stood, were part of Strafford's advice to Charles in the previous year, during the Scottish war. The Secretary of the King's Council, Sir Harry Vane the Elder, twice deposed on oath that he could not remember any words of Strafford's urging the King to use the Irish army to subdue opposition in England. It was only on a third examination that he declared Strafford to have said, 'You have an Army in Ireland which you may employ here, to reduce this Kingdom'. 'This kingdom'—Scotland or England? It was only when the impeachment was obviously failing and the opposition were considering a Bill of Attainder that a copy of the notes taken at the Council meeting conveniently turned up: even so their ambiguity remained. It was at this point that Digby, who had previously taken an active part in the prosecution of Strafford, intervened. The reader may care to have a longer extract from his speech than could conveniently be introduced into the lecture.

The first time he [Vane] was questioned to all the Interrogatories, and to that part of the Seventh, which concerns the Army of *Ireland*: He said positively in these words, *I cannot Charge him with that*. But for the rest, he desires time to recollect himself, which was granted him.

Some days after he was Examined a second time, and then deposes these words, concerning the King's being Absolved from Rules of Government, and so forth, very clearly. But being prest to that part, concerning the *Irish* Army, He said again, *I can say nothing to that*.

Here we thought we had done with him, till divers weeks after, my Lord of *Northumberland*, and all others of the *Junto*, denying to have heard any thing concerning those words, Of reducing *England* by the *Irish* Army. It was thought fit to Examine the Secretary once more, and then he deposes these words to have been said by the Earl of *Strafford* to His Majesty, *You have an Army in* Ireland, *which you may Imploy here, to reduce* (or some word to that sense) *this Kingdom*.

Mr Speaker, these are the Circumstances which, I confess

with my Conscience, thrust quite out of doors that Grand Article of our Charge, concerning his desperate Advice to the King, of Employing the *Irish* Army here.

Let not this, I beseech you, be driven to an Aspersion upon Mr Secretary, as if he should have Sworn otherwise than he knew or believed; He is too worthy to do that; only let thus much be inferred from it, that he, who twice upon Oath, with time of recollection, could not remember any thing of such a business, might well a third time mis-remember somewhat in this business, the difference of one letter, here for there, or that for this, quite alters the Case, the latter also being more probable, since it is confest of all hands, that the Debate then was concerning a War with *Scotland*; and you may remember, that at the Bar he once said, To employ there. And thus, Mr Speaker, I have faithfully given you an account what it is that hath blunted the edge of the Hatchet or Bill with me towards my Lord of *Strafford*.

This was that whereupon I Accused him with a free heart, Prosecuted him with earnestness, and had it, to my understanding, been proved, should have condemned him with Innocence. Whereas now I cannot satisfie my Conscience to do it.

I profess, I can have no notion of any bodies intent to subvert the Laws Treasonably, or by force; and this design of Force not appearing, all his other wicked Practises cannot amount so high with me.

I can find a more easie and more natural Spring, from whence to derive all his other Crimes, than from an intent to bring in Tyranny, and to make his own Posterity, as well as Us, Slaves; as from Revenge, from Pride, from Avarice, from Passion, and Insolence of Nature.

But had this of the *Irish* Army been proved, it would have diffused a Complexion of Treason over all, it would have been a Withe, indeed, to bind all those other scattered and lesser branches, as it were, into a Faggot of Treason.

I do not say but the rest may represent him a man as worthy to die, but perhaps worthier than many a Traytor. I do not say, but they may justly direct Us to Enact, That they shall be Treason for the future.

But God keep me from giving Judgment of Death on any man, and of Ruine to his innocent Posterity, upon a Law made *a Posteriori*.

Let the Mark be set on the door where the Plague is, and then let him that will enter die.

I know, Mr Speaker, there is in Parliament, a double Power of Life and Death by Bill, a Judicial Power, and a Legislative; the measure of the one, is what's legally just; of the other, what is Prudentially and Politickly fit for the good and preservation of the whole. But these two, under favour, are not to be confounded in Judgment: We must not piece up want of legality with matter of convenience, not the defailance of prudential fitness with a pretence of legal Justice.

To Condemn my Lord of *Strafford* Judicially, as for Treason, my Conscience is not assured that the matter will bear it.

And I do it by the Legislative Power, my reason consultively cannot agree to that, since I am perswaded, neither the Lords nor the King will pass the Bill, and consequently that Our passing it will be a Cause of great Divisions and Combustions in the State.

And therefore my humble advice is, That laying aside this Bill of Attainder, We may think of another, saving only Life, such as may secure the State from my Lord of *Strafford*, without endangering it, as much by Division concerning his Punishment, as he hath endangered it by his Practices.

If this may not be hearkned unto, Let me conclude, in saying that unto you all, which I have throughly inculcated to mine own Conscience upon this occasion. Let every man lay his hand upon his Heart, and sadly consider what We are going to do, with a Breath, either Justice or Murther; Justice on the one side, or Murther heightned and aggravated to its supreamest extent. For as the *Casuists* say, That he who lies with his Sister commits Incest, but he that marries his Sister sins higher, by applying God's Ordinance to his Crime: So doubtless he that commits Murther with the Sword of Justice, heightens that Crime to the utmost.

The danger being so great, and the Case so doubtful, that I

see the best Lawyers in diametral opposition concerning it:
Let every man wipe his Heart, as he does his Eyes, when he
would Judge of a nice and subtile Object. The Eye if it be
pretincted with any colour, is vitiated in its discerning. Let
Us take heed of a blood-shotten Eye in Judgment.

Let every man purge his Heart clear of all passions, (I
know this great and wise Body-politick can have none, but I
speak to individuals, from the weakness which I find in my
self) away with personal Animosities, away with all flatteries
to the people, in being the sharper against him, because he is
odious to them; away with all fears, lest by the sparing his
blood they may be incens'd; away with all such Considerations, as that it is not fit for a Parliament, that one Accused
by it of Treason, should escape with Life.

Let not former Vehemence of any against him, nor fear
from thence, that he cannot be safe while that man lives, be
an ingredient in the Sentence of any one of Us.

Of all these Corruptives of Judgment, Mr Speaker, I do
before God discharge my self to the uttermost of my power.

And do with a clear Conscience wash my hands of this
mans blood, by this solemn Protestation, That my Vote goes
not to the taking of the Earl of *Strafford*'s Life.

The quality of the speech comes out if we compare it with the
rhetorical heightening employed by Pym on the second day of the
proceedings:

It is the cause of the Kingdom. It concerns not only the Peace
and Prosperity, but even the Being of the Kingdom. We have
that piercing Eloquence, the Cries and Groans, and Tears,
and Prayers of all the subjects assisting us. We have the three
Kingdoms, *England*, and *Scotland*, and *Ireland* in Travail
and Agitation with us, bowing themselves, like the *Hindes*
spoken of in *Job*, to cast out their Sorrows.

I suppose that in an opening speech for the prosecution one
shouldn't be surprised to find this sort of thing. But it does compare

very unfavourably with the straightforward sincerity of Digby's speech.*

7 (see page 41)

He does, of course: the new king tells him near the end of the play,

> Thy pains, Fitzwater, shall not be forgot;
> Right noble is thy merit, well I wot—

which may be simply bad writing, but is more likely to represent a dry irony.

8 (see page 42)

Menenius says of the Tribunes, 'You wear out a good wholesome forenoon in hearing a cause between an orange-wife and a forset-seller, and then rejourn the controversy of three-pence to a second day of audience'. Self-importance? Well, perhaps. But it is precisely the patience of Escalus in *Measure for Measure* (II, i) in sifting an apparently trivial case, that establishes him as a just and sympathetic figure.

9 (see page 43)

Anton Ehrenzweig, in *The Hidden Order of Art*, speaks of the great artist's ability to relax his attention, to risk losing his firm grasp of an habitual manner of dealing with his 'material', so that promptings from the unconscious—or at any rate from beyond the fixed structure of the ego—may enter into the process of new creation. A passage from his book may be quoted here for its bearing on the matters touched on in the text.

> One cannot separate creativity from its social basis. . . . A
> frequent failure in human relationships is due to the same

* *The Tryal of Thomas Earl of Strafford . . . upon an Impeachment of High Treason*; Rushworth, *Historical Collections*, Vol. VIII, pp. 52-3, 103. The impeachment and attainder are vividly described by Miss C. V. Wedgwood in *Thomas Wentworth, First Earl of Strafford, 1593-1641*, Part III, Chapters iii-v.

ego rigidity that impedes creativity. We have to give our substance freely, project it into other people or creative work for further transformation. As in creative work we must be humble and grateful to receive back far more than we ourselves have put in. Our personality will grow through this creative interchange, which underlies the metabolism of our social life. . . . Creativity, then, may be self-creation, but it is possible only through social intercourse, whether with other individuals as happens in social creativity in the narrower sense of the word, or through the medium of impersonal creative work.—*The Hidden Order of Art* (Paladin paperback edition), p. 235.

10 (see page 44)

This is a pattern that will be repeated in the last Act, but then with Bolingbroke occupying the throne. It is a neat reversal, but the questions raised at the beginning concerning the relation of royal power to justice and right action still remain.

11 (see page 46)

See, for example, Norma Dolbie Solve, *Stuart Politics in Chapman's 'Tragedy of Chabot'*; Peter Ure, 'Chapman's Tragedies', *Stratford-upon-Avon Studies, 1, Jacobean Theatre* (ed. John Russell Brown and Bernard Harris); K. M. Burton, 'The Political Tragedies of Chapman and Ben Jonson', *Essays in Criticism*, Vol. II, 1952, pp. 397-412; Edwin Muir, 'Royal Man: Notes on the Tragedies of Chapman', in *Essays on Literature and Society*.

T. M. Parrott, in his Introduction to *The Tragedy of Chabot* (Chapman, *The Tragedies*, pp. 613 ff.), sees the tragedies as rehearsing the coming struggle between the claims of absolutist government and the rights of the individual. The Byron plays proclaim that 'the days of unrestrained individualism were over . . . *Chabot* is no less a solemn warning to the absolute monarchs of the new age. . . . The lesson of the tragedy is the necessity for the free play of the individual within the limits of the state organism, or, to put it more concretely, the duty of the absolute monarch to respect the liberty of the loyal subject. This was a lesson at once needed and unheeded by Chapman's own kings, James and Charles, and its neglect was one of the prime causes which brought about within a generation the tragic downfall of the ancient monarchy of England.'

An even more interesting case is argued by G. R. Hibbard, in 'George Chapman: Tragedy and the Providential View of History' (*Shakespeare Survey*, 20, 1967). Just as in the early seventeenth century there was a movement away from the 'providential' view of history towards a more objective presentation of events, so the Jacobean tragic writers showed 'what men do, not what they ought to do'. Chapman, with his strong moral sense, was caught in a dilemma. Only *Chabot* comes near to meeting the demands of poetic justice. 'The strength of the other tragedies comes, at least in part, . . . from the fact that they embody other attitudes to history and to human life which cut across the providential one.' Chapman saw 'that many of the great conflicts of history arise, not out of the clash of right with wrong, but of right with right'. The result is a sense of tragic conflict in public action that is prophetic of the later course of English history and links Chapman with both Clarendon and Marvell.

A recent re-reading of Chapman left me unconvinced. It's not only that his characters lack depth, but that his language doesn't engage with, or open up towards, the complex world that even the most resolute individualists have to come to terms with. It is for this reason that his heroes so often seem to be striking moral attitudes in empty space: as Edwin Muir says, they 'wander about . . . enclosed in a dream of greatness'. There is *conflict* in Chapman between his obvious desire to endorse the man of heroic self-assertion (Bussy, Byron) and his desire to endorse the 'Senecal' man who rejects the world and relies solely on his own virtue and fortitude (Clermont). But this isn't the same thing as the recognition of complexity; nor does it support the claim that Chapman was aware of the nascent constitutional conflict. Indeed I have come to think that Chapman's main significance in the political world of the seventeenth century is as a portent, inasmuch as his violent simplifications encourage an attitude towards public affairs that is decidedly not Marvellian. This is not to deny that he does, in his queer way, represent a good deal that was working in 'the mind of the age'; but he is, I think, symptomatic, without possessing the insights that have been attributed to him.

I regret that Dr J. W. Lever's *The Tragedy of State*—which considers 'Jacobean tragedy as a product of the intellectual ferment and spiritual upheaval which preceded the first great European revolution'—appeared too late for me to use it in the preparation of Chapter II.

12 (see page 48)

It is an acute remark of Professor Harry Levin's that for Jonson, 'always more interested in human machinations than in the workings of destiny, tragedy could be reduced to conspiracy'. —'Two Magian Comedies: "The Tempest" and "The Alchemist" ', *Shakespeare Survey*, 22. Professor Levin also remarks that 'Shakespeare's attitudes towards human nature were animated by sympathetic curiosity, even as Jonson's were by acute suspicion'.

13 (see page 49)

In *Coriolanus* it is, as we should expect, the patricians who rely most on abstractions: the plebs naturally use the language of direct sensation. To take a single example: at II, ii, 84, Cominius appeals to what is for him a self-evident truth—'It is held / That valour is the chiefest virtue . . .' Shakespeare of course knew that in the list of the cardinal virtues fortitude (which may include, but can't simply be equated with, valour) came after justice, prudence and temperance: in *Macbeth* (IV, ii, 91-4) the king-becoming graces are listed 'As justice, verity, temperance . . . fortitude'. But there is no need to look outside the play to find that Shakespeare took a rather critical view of Cominius' article of faith. We can no more avoid the pointed association between Caius Marcius' bravery (which is not denied) and the expenditure of life-giving blood from human veins than we can avoid the descriptions of warfare in terms of a misplaced sexuality. It is an odd kind of 'chiefest virtue' that so often brings with it suggestions of a nightmare: Marcius 'does appear as he were flay'd' (I, vi, 23), he boasts to Aufidius, ' 'tis not *my* blood / Wherein thou seest me mask'd' (I, viii, 9), and Cominius describes him in battle, 'from face to foot / He was a thing of blood . . . he did / Run reeking o'er the lives of men' (II, ii, 109 ff.). It is all very well for Volumnia to depersonalize the animal fury of the man in battle—'Death, that dark spirit, in's nervy arm does lie . . .'—the play reminds us (and through Coriolanus himself) of the consequences in simple human terms:

> A goodly city is this Antium. City,
> 'Tis I that made thy widows: many an heir
> Of these fair edifices 'fore my wars
> Have I heard groan and drop . . .
>
> (IV, iv, 1 ff.)

It is perhaps worth remarking, with relation to the disguising function of generalisations, that Coriolanus—in a scene immediately following the exhibition of an ungarnished traitor—presents to himself his treacherous intentions as though they were unlucky happenings over which he had no control: see the speech beginning, 'O world, thy slippery turns! . . . ' (IV, iv, 12 ff.)

In what I have written in the text above I am concious of a general debt to William Empson's *The Structure of Complex Words*.

14 (see page 54)

Christopher Morris, *Political Thought in England: Tyndale to Hooker* (Home University Library), p. 189. Peter Munz, in *The Place of Hooker in the History of Thought*, Chapter ii, writes well of what reason meant to Hooker. 'Reason to him was not only a mechanical process that could also be performed by a calculating machine. The meaning of reason was to him the same as it had been in the Middle Ages and in Antiquity: it implied an intuitive as well as a discursive element . . . according to this conception, the powers of reason were enormously wide and varied' (p. 64).

15 (see page 55)

The Puritan error is to think that the *only* law of God is that contained in the Bible—'that Scripture is the only rule of all things which in this life may be done'—and that anything not explicitly commanded there is forbidden. 'Admit this, and what shall the Scripture be but a snare and a torment to weak consciences, filling them with infinite perplexities, scrupulosities, doubts insoluble, and extreme despairs?' (Book II, viii, 6).

16 (see page 57)

A. P. d'Entrèves, *The Medieval Contribution to Political Thought*, Chapter vi, p. 125. And of course, as in the medieval tradition, thinking about politics is removed from a narrowly defined realm of 'the political'; its roots are in religion, and the State can never be an end in itself. 'For if the course of politic affairs cannot in any sort go forward without fit instruments, and that which fitteth them be their virtues, let Polity acknowledge itself indebted to Religion; godliness being the chiefest top and wellspring of all true virtues, even as God himself is of all good things. So natural is the union of Religion with Justice, that we may boldly deem there is neither, where both are not. . . . If they, which employ their labour and travel about the public administration of justice, follow it only as a trade, with unquenchable and unconscionable thirst of gain, being not in heart persuaded that justice is God's own work, and themselves his agents in this business . . . formalities of justice do but serve to smother right, and that, which was necessarily ordained for the common good, is through shameful abuse made the cause of common misery' (V, i, 2).

17 (see page 61)

Perez Zagorin, *The Court and the Country* (Routledge and Kegan Paul, 1969), pp. 55-6 and *passim*. Professor Zagorin also brings out the conservative nature of the opposition to the Court in the thirty or forty years preceding the Civil War.

> The Country was a conservative opposition. Its adherents had no prejudice in favour of change. Certainly, in contesting with James I and Charles I, they did not set out to alter the government. They felt no necessity to rationalize a new version of the state or the English constitution because they conceived themselves defenders of an immemorial legal order of rights and liberties against which the King was the transgressor. He, not his antagonists, was the innovator—so it seemed to the Country (p. 83).

Conservative dislike of Stuart policy is seen in Fulke Greville's *Life of Sir Philip Sidney*, which, perhaps significantly, was not published until 1652.

18 (see page 66)

And the techniques of academic disputation at Cambridge: see William Riley Parker, *Milton: a Biography*, Vol. I, pp. 51-2. Those interested in the ways in which rhetoric was cultivated at the universities in the early part of the century may consult Hacket's *Life* of Archbishop Williams (*Scrinia Reserata*, 1693), pp. 16-18. The modern reader must feel that there was something excessive in the admiration that an able man could win by a display of his mastery of the traditional forms.

19 (see page 69)

I have not done justice to *A Ready and Easy Way*, with its noble, rather touching, though still simplifying view of the right way for a nation to obtain its proper governors. The man who wrote it, however, had a *right* to disillusion. On 'political patience' and *Samson Agonistes*, see M. A. Radzinowicz, ' "Samson Agonistes" and Milton the Politician in Defeat', *Philological Quarterly*, Supplement to Vol. XLIV (1965), pp. 454 ff.

20 (see page 73)

Since I have not read this work I cannot pronounce on it; but it is clear from the long account in W. K. Jordan's monumental *Development of Religious Toleration in England* (the second volume of which contains a good introduction to the thought of the Latitudinarians) that for Chillingworth the essentials of Christianity were few and simple, and that persecution in religion was an absolute evil. Indeed, according to Jordan, 'Chillingworth came very near to saying that even the fundamental truths could not be exactly defined. He could do no more than define belief in the fundamentals as the honest and dispassionate search for truth, for, he held, any man who so searches will necessarily find saving truth. He regarded the Bible as the sole authority in religion, but at the same time insisted upon the complete liberty of the individual to interpret Holy Writ as his reason should dictate. In the final analysis reason remains the sole judge in religious controversies.'— *The Development of Religious Toleration in England, 1603-1640*, p. 396. For the tolerant strain in Puritanism, see A. S. P. Woodhouse, *Puritanism and Liberty*, Introduction, pp. 45-7, and William Haller, *The Rise of Puritanism* (Harper Torchbooks), pp. 195 ff.

21 (see page 75)

B. H. G. Wormald, *Clarendon: Politics, Historiography and Religion*, p. 82. His position remained the same after the war had started. 'Throughout the period from 1641 to the Treaty of Uxbridge, Hyde, as a public figure, had but one aim, to heal the breach between the King and the two Houses of Parliament. . . . But, despite increasingly complex circumstances, bridge-building is the explanation of his thoughts and actions throughout this whole period.'—Wormald, *op. cit.*, p. 150. Compare Professor Trevor-Roper's view that Clarendon 'was at his best both in politics and in literature, as a conciliator. If any man could have reconciled King and Parliament in the critical years 1640-2 it was Clarendon: when the breach was irreparable his influence declined, but we can trace it still, in his state papers, reconciling, with infinite tact and understanding, mutually suspicious groups of exiles and conspirators. His greatest work in politics—the Restoration Settlement—was again a work of conciliation.'—'Clarendon and the Great Rebellion', *Historical Essays*, p. 248.

22 (see page 86)

Burke, allowing his constitutional ideals to shape what he saw in France, almost paraphrases this passage. 'In your old states [States-General] you possessed that variety of parts corresponding with the various descriptions of which your community was happily composed; you had all that combination, and all that opposition of interests, you had that action and counteraction which, in the natural and in the political world, from the reciprocal struggle of discordant powers, draws out the harmony of the universe. These opposed and conflicting interests, which you considered as so great a blemish in your old and in our present constitution, interpose a salutary check to all precipitate resolutions; they render deliberation a matter not of choice, but of necessity; they make all change a subject of *compromise*, which naturally begets moderation; they produce *temperaments*, preventing the sore evil of harsh, crude, unqualified reformations; and rendering all the headlong exertions of arbitrary power, in the few or in the many, for ever impracticable. Through that diversity of members and interests, general liberty had as many securities as there were separate views in the several orders; whilst by pressing down the whole by the weight of a real monarchy, the separate parts would have been prevented from warping and starting from their allotted places.'—*Reflections on the Revolution in France*, ed. Conor Cruise O'Brien (Penguin), p. 122.

23 (see page 101)

Similarly, although the Presbyterians had shown themselves tyrannical and some of the sects had a fanatic fringe, Dryden's contemptuous dismissal of *all* Nonconformity ('The swelling poison of the several sects') may be seen as excessive. The 'numerous host of dreaming saints' did, after all, include a Bunyan.

24 (see page 105)

Perez Zagorin, *The Court and the Country*, p. 9. The results of the French Revolution—after Jacobinism, the dictatorship of Napoleon and the Bourbon Restoration—have been summed up by Professor Cobban: 'A class of officials and professional men moved up from the minor to major posts in government and dispossessed the minions of an effete Court: this was what the bourgeois revolution meant. The peasants relieved themselves of their seigneural dues: this was the meaning of the abolition of feudalism. But even taken together these two developments hardly constitute the abolition of one social order and the substitution of another for it, and if the accepted theory is not quite a myth it seems singularly like one.'—*The Myth of the French Revolution*, p. 20.

25 (see page 105)

In Russia in the twentieth century the Revolution, at enormous human cost, hastened the industrialization of an economically backward country; but it was from the exigencies of the first revolutionary years that modern Russia (with whatever basic differences within the Communist party) inherited its present tradition of centralized and bureaucratic control.

26 (see page 106)

He has some notable pages on the 'panic of property' and 'the errors of the Aristocratic party . . . full as gross, and far less excusable'. And he warned his readers that 'in recoiling with too incautious an abhorrence from the bugbears of innovation, they may sink all at once into the slough of slavishness and corruption. Let such persons recollect that the charms of hope and novelty furnish some palliatives for the idolatry to which *they* seduce the mind; but that the apotheosis of familiar abuses . . . is the vilest of superstition.'

27 (see page 108)

Biographia Literaria, ed. Shawcross, Vol. I, p. 19, Vol. II, p. 117; *Essays on his own Times*, Vol. II, p. 543. As Miss Hannah Arendt has recently remarked: 'It is always the same old story: being taken in by every catchword, the inability to think or else the unwillingness to see phenomena as they really are, without applying categories to them in the belief that they can thereby be classified. It is just this that constitutes theoretical helplessness.' —'Thoughts on Politics and Revolution', *New York Review of Books*, April 22, 1971, p. 12.

28 (see page 112)

Thus, 'the objective content of the word "deviationist" puts it into a penological category. If two deviationists band together, they become "fractionists", which does not involve an objectively different crime, but an increase in the sentence imposed.' Barthes also remarks that 'a history of political modes of writing would . . . be the best of social phenomenologies'.—*Writing Degree Zero* (translated from the French by Annette Lavers and Colin Smith), pp. 30-1.